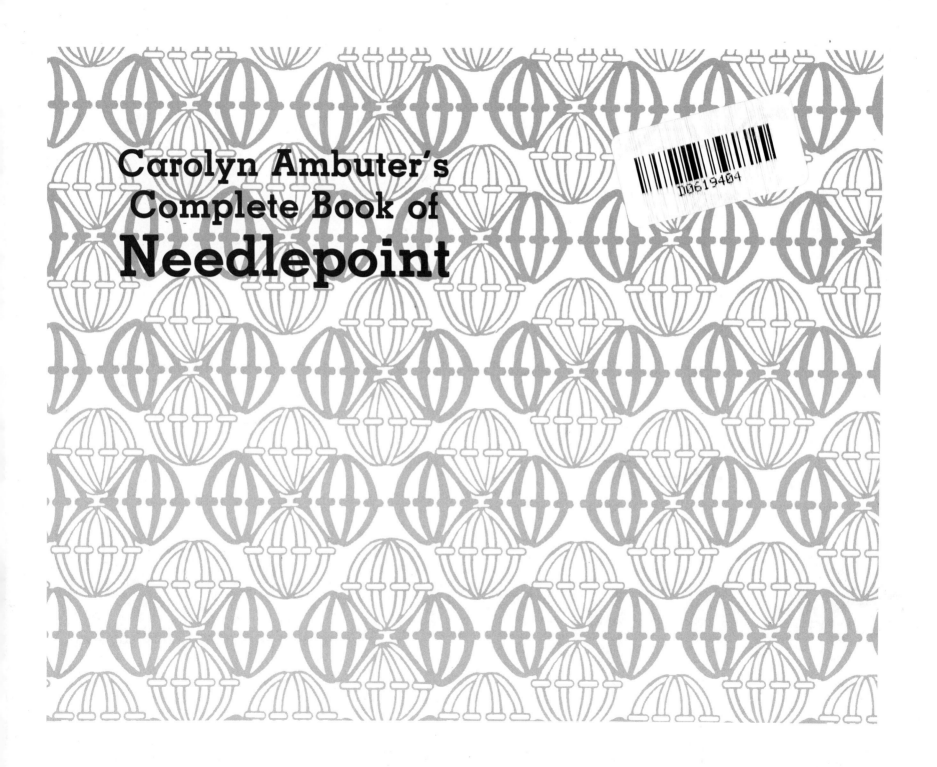

Carolyn Ambuter's
Complete Book of
Needlepoint

Workman Publishing Company Inc.

Carolyn Ambuter's Complete Book of **Needlepoint**

Illustrated by Patti Baker Russell
Photographs by Fred Samperi

Thomas Y. Crowell Company
New York 10022   Established 1834

Published by Thomas Y. Crowell Company
in conjunction with Workman Publishing Company
Published in Canada by Fitzhenry & Whiteside Limited, Toronto
ISBN 0-690-00337-4
Library of Congress catalog card number: 70-178814
Printed in the United States of America
photographs by Fred Samperi

10 9 8 7 6 5 4

Preface

As a shopkeeper, I have tangled with many phases of canvas work, from the nitty gritty to the divine. I have often wished I had a handy reference book in which I could hastily refresh my memory on how to form one of the many stitches or how many ply to use on a particular canvas, and to which I could refer customers anxious to paint their own designs or set up their own Florentine Embroidery. That I should write such a book seemed remote. But one day I was asked to do just that—to assemble a needlepoint compendium that would serve as both a primer for the beginner and a reference book for the advanced needlepointer. Here I have tried to answer all the questions that I have been asked and to supply all the information an avid needlepointer needs.

CAROLYN AMBUTER

Acknowledgments

My heartfelt thanks to my husband Joe, my daughter Jean, and my dear friends and co-workers Sue Fiordelisi, Patti Russell, and Sherry Gordon for their constant efforts, encouragement, and artistic contributions that are reflected in this book. More warm thanks to Ann Bramson who so cheerfully and carefully edited this book.

I would also like to express my appreciation to all the people who made contributions without knowing they were doing so; the authors of the many books on canvas work and embroidery that I have freely consumed, the lessons I studied from the National Council of American Embroiderers, and the customers who came to my shop and from whom I learned so much by helping them solve their needlepoint problems.

It is my sincerest wish that this book will aid and inspire others in turn, and it is to this desire that this book is dedicated.

Contents

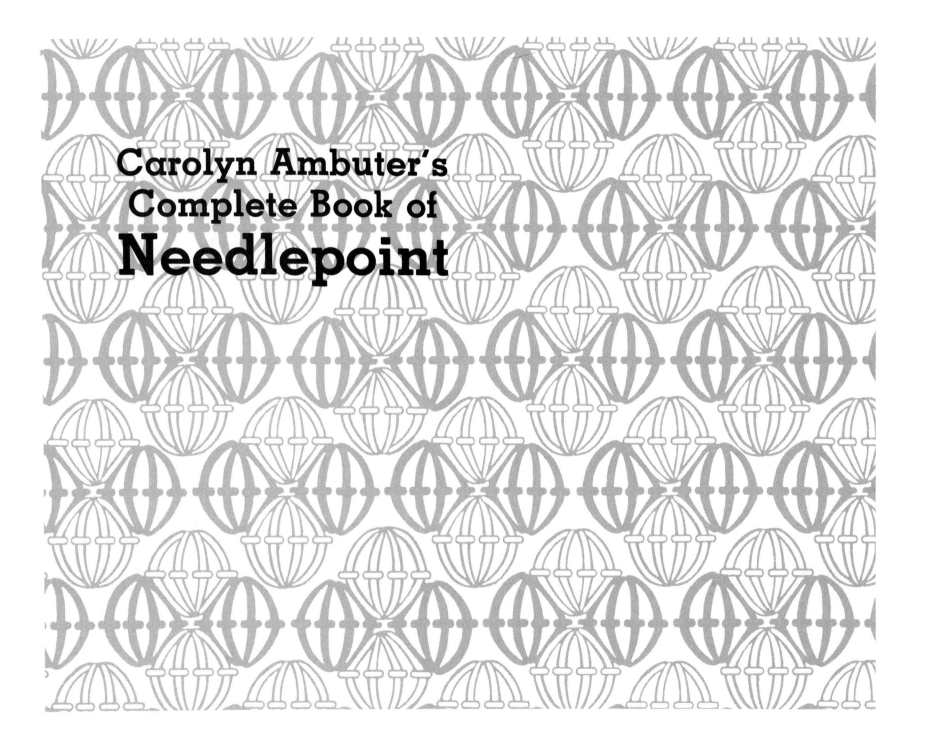

Carolyn Ambuter's
Complete Book of
Needlepoint

Working Materials

Canvas

Canvas is the open-weave fabric on which you work. It is the skeleton of the finished piece on which you will spend many pleasant hours stitching.

Mono canvas   There are two basic types of canvas, each comes in a variety of sizes. Mono canvas is the type most frequently used today. It is constructed of single horizontal threads crossed by single vertical threads.

Penelope canvas   Penelope canvas is the other type. It has two horizontal threads crossing two closely woven vertical threads. The advantage of this double-threaded canvas is that you can work the details of a complex pattern in tiny (petit point) stitches and the background in larger (gros point) stitches. Petit point is done by pricking apart the vertical canvas threads. The horizontal and vertical threads are used individually, thus making it possible to take four petit point stitches in an area that previously accommodated only one gros point stitch.

After working a few mono canvases, a true needlepointer will want to try her hand with a penelope canvas, beginning with petit point and then trying some of the many other stitches in mini size.

Mesh size   Both mono and penelope canvas come in different mesh gauges which determine the size of the stitches. A mesh is the intersection of a horizontal and vertical canvas thread. Stitches are taken over the mesh. When we speak of a 10-mesh canvas, we mean 10 mesh or 10 stitches to the inch. The fewer mesh to the inch, the larger the stitches and the fewer stitches needed to cover a given area. The more mesh to the inch, the smaller the stitches and the more stitches required to cover the canvas.

Mono canvas is available in 10, 12, 14, 16, 18, 20, and 24 mesh to the inch. For the beginner, I would suggest working on 10- or 12-mesh mono. Penelope canvas is indicated by two numbers, such as 10/20. The first is the number of gros point mesh to the

24-mesh mono

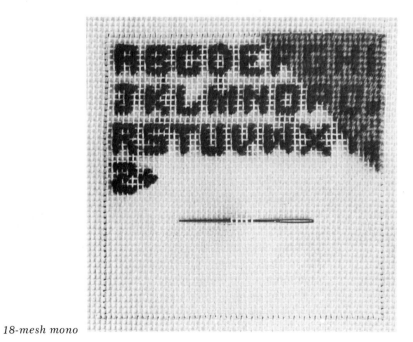

18-mesh mono

1

16-mesh mono

14-mesh mono

inch; the second refers to the number of petit point mesh. The most readily available is 10/20; 11/22, 12/24, and 14/28 are also obtainable, but you will have to search for them. There are also 5-, 4-, and 3½-mesh penelope rug canvases. Although these canvases have double threads, they are not generally used for petit point, hence the one number size. (The double threads can be split, however, for an interesting petit point and gros point effect. The gros point may be done in a big stitch with rug wool and the petit point in strands of Persian.) The double threads give strength to the widely spaced mesh.

Canvas colors Most mono canvas is white, except for the very fine petit point canvases of 18 and 24 mesh that are often peach color. There is an excellent quality tan mono canvas that is suitable for counted work—Florentine Embroidery or work from graphed designs. The tan tone makes any "grin-through" (spots of canvas peeping out between rows of stitches) less apparent. Unfortunately, it is not easy to obtain.

Penelope canvas is usually tan. A white penelope

is available, but with the exception of a 10/20 mesh, it is not always of the best quality.

Quality At one time the choicest canvas was made of linen. Now only cotton is used for even the best canvases. Though there are some adequate canvases from other countries, I have found the quality of the French ones superior.

It is not a good idea to economize on canvas. Poor quality canvases may be too harsh or too limp. A harsh canvas tears at the wool as it passes through the mesh opening. Your canvas should have smooth, polished threads that allow the yarn to flow freely by them. Polished threads also resist being split by the tapestry needle or being knicked by a scissors when ripping.

The threads of a limp canvas make for uneven stitches, particularly for a beginner who has not yet developed an even tension. The starched body of a canvas controls the regularity of the stitches. However, an overly stiff canvas often becomes overly limp when worked.

12-mesh mono

10-mesh mono

A fragile canvas should be resisted by all but the most experienced needlepointers, who may on account of its fragility select it for a special project. Because it is practically a gauze, special care must be given in the blocking and mounting so that the thin threads are not broken.

Knots　Choice quality canvas will have knots. Large knots may leave lumps in the stitching, and there is also the danger of the knots coming apart in the blocking of the finished piece of work. When purchasing canvas by the yard or part of the yard, buy a piece large enough so that these knots can be avoided or be positioned in the margins of the worked area. Knots rarely occur in quality handpainted canvases, as they have been carefully skirted. When doing a one-piece rug of any size, it is literally impossible to acquire a piece of mono canvas without knots. Apply a little white glue over the knots as a precaution.

Yarns

Needlepoint yarns are selected for their suitability for canvas work. They must be strong enough to take the repeated pulling through the mesh openings, the tugging of blocking, and the long, hard wear of an heirloom. Knitting wools are unsatisfactory because they are springy and elastic—qualities to be desired in knitting but not in needlepoint. Knitting wools also wear too quickly, get fuzzy, and tend to pill. A good needlepoint yarn should have very little springiness to it so that a stitch remains in place exactly as it is laid with the needle.

Persian wool　The most popular and practical needlepoint wool on the market is Persian wool. The finest Persian is made by the Paternayan Brothers. This is the same type of wool that is used in the making of Persian rugs. Although it does not come exclusively from Persia, it does come from cool, mountainous regions where the sheep grow tough, long hair and where there are plenty of trees for them to rub their coats against. These conditions produce the luster that is peculiar to this type of wool. Persian has a great deal of character when worked—a slightly hairy quality combined with a soft sheen. Like Persian rugs, Persian needlepoint seems to grow more beautiful with age and wear.

Each strand of Persian is composed of 3 plies. It can be adapted to different size meshes by taking away plies or adding to them. A 10-mesh canvas uses the full strand for a Tent Stitch. A 12- or 14-mesh canvas uses 2 plies. (Suggested plies for other mesh sizes appear on the Canvas Chart on page 8.) The 3 plies are easily separated by gently pulling one ply away from the others. Odd single plies are paired and then used.

Persian comes in all the lovely soft colors of old Persian rugs and natural dyes. There are over three hundred shades which include many color families, sometimes as many as seven values of one color, sometimes four or five.

Laine Colbert There is a French version of Persian wool called Laine Colbert which somewhat resembles Persian.

Tapestry yarn Tapestry yarn looks like a tightly spun knitting worsted. It is smoother than Persian, but because it is made from shorter hairs it doesn't have its silklike sheen. During the "dark ages" of needlepoint (from the first part of this century through the second World War) this was the only needlepoint wool generally available. It was used to fill in the background of preworked canvases. It is still available; domestic tapestry wool comes in 40-yard skeins and imported varieties come in small pull skeins. The imported yarns offer a wide variety of colors. Coats Anchor Tapisserie wool from England and DMC Laine Tapisserie from France are both very good.

Tapestry wool works smoothly on 10 or 12 mesh in the Tent Stitch. One advantage of this wool is that it comes in consistent dye lots. If you run out of wool, you can go back to any shop that carries it and your colors will match exactly.

Nantucket Twist Nantucket Twist is a welcome addition to the collection of needlepoint yarns. The texture resembles that

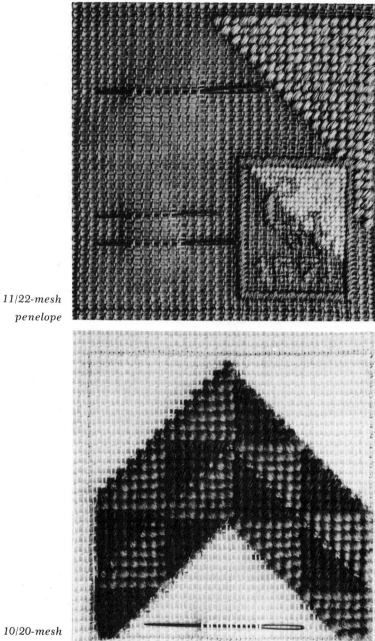

11/22-mesh penelope

10/20-mesh penelope

4

of tapestry wool because it is twisted, but it is made of long imported fibers and has more character than tapestry wool. Each strand is composed of 4 plies and a full strand is suitable for Tent Stitch on a 12- or 14-mesh canvas. It is very convenient, when using either of these popular canvas sizes, to be able to use a full strand of yarn, without having to separate plies as would be necessary with Persian.

Nantucket Twist is particularly valuable for fine canvas work because of the thinness of each ply; 2 plies cover an 18-mesh canvas to perfection where 1 ply of Persian is skimpy and 2 plies are too heavy. Another virtue of this wool is a color range of over one hundred and thirty colors. The colors are mainly clear bright hues.

Crewel

Crewel wool is a pleasant, fine-textured wool most often used for embroidering fabric. Most crewel wool is a little more springy than desired for needlepoint, but because it is so fine it works well in petit point (16 or more stitches to the inch). Crewel wools vary in weight and the number of strands used in the needle must be adjusted to the openings in the mesh. It is possible to purchase crewel yarn in small tubes or wound on cards in small amounts.

Rug wool

Rug wool is a fat, rough-textured wool that is so very quick to work that canvases using rug wool are often dubbed "quick point." The big stitches on large-holed mesh are a treat for tired or sick eyes. It is an excellent selection for the very young or old — or those who want to complete a project in a hurry.

Silk

Every needlepointer should at one time attempt working with a bit of silk, not only for the sheer luxury of it — it is the most costly of yarns — but also for the delight in selecting colors. There is a luminous quality to silk that makes the colors glow. Silk yarns for canvas work come from England and France. English silk is shinier and tends to be more difficult to work than French silk, which has an elegant satin luster and works quite smoothly. French silk has a

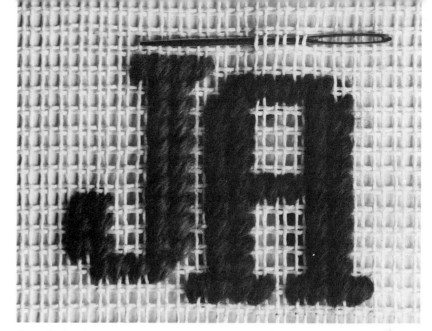

5-mesh penelope

further advantage of coming in 7 plies which can be readily separated and adjusted to any size canvas.

Silk is rarely used for a whole canvas but rather for details and highlights: faces worked in petit point, butterflies, insects, flowers, and some shades in a Florentine design are all choice occasions for silk thread. It is easiest to use in small areas where it can be anchored in the wool nearby. Anchoring silk in silk is a task. Plies of silk are apt to separate and it is necessary to stroke the strands every so often. French silk should not be blocked in the usual fashion. Not all colors are colorfast and the shine is lost in the wetting. A steaming on the back of the work only is recommended.

French linen

Like silk, the most beautiful linen thread comes from France. Unlike French silk, the color selection is limited to what could be called background colors. Though this yarn appears to come in plies, it cannot be separated satisfactorily. It is easily worked in a Tent Stitch on a 12-mesh canvas. It is used in a Back Stitch for the background of My Vest, page 38. Since it was selected to team with the natural canvas color of the vest, it is an added attraction to have some

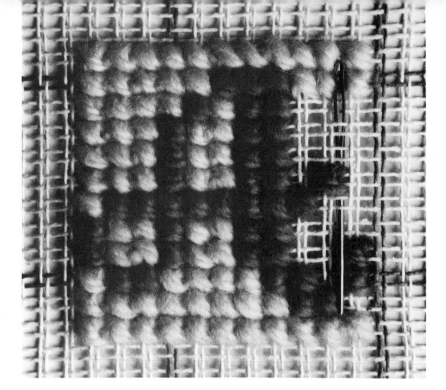

4-mesh penelope

3½-mesh penelope

canvas thread exposed, as it gives a hand-loomed appearance.

It is most important to keep the linen flat and untwisted, stroking the threads when necessary and twisting the needle in the oppostie direction of the twist while stitching.

Metallics, rayon, and novelties

I am purposely including metallics with novelties as I feel that for most needlepoint pieces they must be used with exquisite taste and judgment or they cheapen the appearance. There are just a few of these metallics that are satisfactory and they must be handled with great care. I suggest that metallics and novelties such as raffia, rayons, and nubby yarns be reserved for experimental pieces or for decorative pieces to be looked at but not handled.

Cottons

Cottons are used in much the same fashion as silks: to add highlights and to create a contrasting texture to the wool. Pearl cotton makes a lovely shiny accent. Cotton may be used alone, but in my estimation it is a poor country cousin when compared to the quiet richness and longevity of wool or the elegance of silk.

Wearability

Persian, tapestry, and Nantucket Twist are all long-wearing wools and excellent choices for chair seats, benches, footstools, handbags, or any other item to receive long and hard wear. For this reason, silk, cotton, metallics, and other novelty threads should be avoided. Reserve them for decorative pieces such as hangings. Many old pieces of needlepoint have areas where cotton or silk were used for shine or high-light, and the canvas is bare in just these areas because they have disintegrated with age.

Fading

It has been my experience that needlepoint wools fade from harsh light and exposure to a bright sun. But it is also true that most needlepoint does not begin to be beautiful until it has had some mellowing and wear. I would not deliberately put a needlepoint pil-low in the sun—as some people do who like a mellow look—but on the other hand I would not worry over fading, for unlike people, needlepoint gets more beautiful with age and wear.

Mothproofing Most yarns on the market today are mothproofed. Persian and tapestry wools and any other fine yarn suggested for needlepoint are no exception.

Washability Washability is another quality to be considered when selecting a needlepoint yarn. Most worked canvases require blocking before mounting. This involves a complete dampening. The yarn must withstand this wetting, as well as future washing or cleaning.

Additional Tools

Needles Tapestry needles are used for needlepoint. They are long-eyed needles with blunt points so as not to split the yarn or the canvas, or prick the fingers. They come in many sizes; like canvas sizing, the finer the needle the higher the number.

The eye of the needle should be large enough to hold the wool or thread comfortably without its slipping out, and the shaft of the needle should be fine enough to draw through the mesh openings without tugging. The Canvas Chart at the end of the chapter gives suggestions for needle sizes for the various canvases and yarns.

When needles get dull, they can be run through an emery. However, it is a good idea to keep a few packages of your favorite sizes on hand.

Thimble Sooner or later you will want a thimble if you are a confirmed needlepointer. The finger that needs it gets quite sore. I prefer the plastic type; the metal ones are apt to slip off. It is necessary to try on a thimble when purchasing it, as they come in sizes.

Scissors I also like to keep two pairs of scissors handy: a really tiny, sharp, pointed pair that will rip stitches easily, and a less dangerous and more friendly one such as a stork scissors for snipping the wool ends. If you are a real do-it-yourself hard-core needlepointer, you will probably want a big pair of shears for cutting canvas and a few extra pairs of fine scissors so you can keep one with each project.

Magnifying glass A magnifying glass is a fun tool to own. It is not a necessity, but it is helpful, particularly when doing petit point or looking for missed stitches. You will also find one useful for studying needlepoint in this book and in others. Especially good for doing petit point is the type of magnifying lens that you can wear suspended from an elastic around your neck. In this way you can work with both hands under the lens.

Working conditions To settle down for an evening's needlepoint, seat yourself in a comfortable chair with adequate back support. A pillow (of needlepoint, of course) tucked in at the lower back makes a chair or sofa with a deep seat more comfortable. Put your feet up on a footstool (another project if you don't have one yet) and begin.

More than adequate light is a necessity, not a luxury. It not only saves errors in stitching and in matching colors but it saves the eyes as well. Rather than a little spotlight on your work, use a lamp with a large spread of bright light directed at your work. I am partial to architect or studio-type lamps which have two kinds of light—incandescent and candescent—such as a Luxo. They are available in art supply and lighting stores. These lamps are flexible and can be easily directed over the work. If you are a confirmed needlepointer, you will probably have several favorite spots for your stitching and each of these places should have its own good light. A right-handed person will find that light coming from over the left shoulder will create less shadow on the work; the left-handed person will find light coming from over the right shoulder is best.

Canvas Chart

SIZE OF MESH	CANVAS DESCRIPTION	TYPE OF YARN	NUMBER OF PLY FOR TENT STITCH	SIZE OF NEEDLE	COMMENTS
mono canvas					
24	peach or white 24 inches wide	Nantucket Twist	1	24	For very delicate designs and lovely thin items such as evening bags, eyeglass cases, neckbands, bookmarks, pockets, cummerbunds, and belts. Don't let the fine canvas frighten you. Most people can work these meshes with glasses or magnifiers. The amount of details and shading possible makes the work most worthwhile. Easy to mount.
		Crewel	1 or 2	22	
		French silk	2	22	
20	peach or white 24 inches wide	Nantucket Twist		22	
		French silk		22	
18	peach or white 24 inches wide	Nantucket Twist	2	22	
		Crewel	1 to 3	22	
		French silk	5	22	
16	white 36 inches wide	Nantucket Twist	3	20	For hard-wearing items with lots of detail such as picture frames, telephone and address books, pillows, and belts.
		Crewel	2 or 3	20	
		French silk	full 7	20	
14	white 36 inches wide	Persian	2	19	An excellent canvas for all purposes. Use 3-ply Persian for Florentine Embroidery.
		Nantucket Twist	full 4	19	
		Tapestry	1	18	
		French silk	full 7	19	
12	white 36 inches wide	Persian	2	18	A good size mesh for all stitches; easy on the eyes but fine enough for some detail.
		Nantucket Twist	full 4	18	
		Tapestry	1	18	
		French silk	full 7	18	
		French linen	full strand	18	
10	white 40 inches wide	Persian	full 3	18	A good selection for beginners and for rugs. Use 4- or 5-ply Persian for Florentine Embroidery.

A note on petit point and gros point. Stitches worked on canvases of 16 or more mesh to the inch are called petit point. Canvases with fewer mesh to the inch are considered gros point. Petit point is most easily worked on mono canvas, either a 16-, 18-, 20-, or 24-mesh canvas depending on the degree of fineness required. However, when petit point is to be used along with gros point, a penelope canvas is selected. To work petit point on a penelope canvas, separate the two vertical canvas threads. Using the tip of the tapestry needle, separate the two threads at the top of the area to be worked. Then drag the needle straight down the canvas between the canvas threads, separating a row at a time. When working petit point in a very small area, the threads can be picked apart individually.

SIZE OF MESH	CANVAS DESCRIPTION	TYPE OF YARN	NUMBER OF PLY FOR TENT STITCH	SIZE OF NEEDLE	COMMENTS

penelope canvas

SIZE OF MESH	CANVAS DESCRIPTION	TYPE OF YARN	NUMBER OF PLY FOR TENT STITCH	SIZE OF NEEDLE	COMMENTS
14/28	tan 36 inches wide	Nantucket Twist	1 for petit point	24	These canvases are not as readily available as the others. The petit point on them is so fine that demand is limited. However, if the eyesight is good, many design possibilities with subtle shading and rendering make these canvases excellent choices. Various stitches may be worked in diminutive size.
			full 4 for gros point	19	
		Persian	2 for gros point	19	
		Tapestry	1 for gros point	18	
		French silk	2 for petit point	24	
			full 7 for gros point	19	
12/24	tan 36 inches wide	Persian	2 for gros point	18	
		Nantucket Twist	1 for petit point	24	
			full 4 for gros point	22	
		Crewel	1 or 2 for petit point	18	
		Tapestry	1 for gros point	18	
		French silk	2 for petit point	22	
			full 7 for gros point	18	
11/22	tan 36 inches wide	Persian	1 for petit point	24	Linen is particularly handsome on this canvas. It keeps the work thin and light, and for this reason is especially good for vests.
			2 or 3 for gros point	18	
		French linen	1 full strand for gros point	18	
		French silk	2 for petit point	22	
10/20	white or tan 36 inches wide	Persian	1 for petit point	24	The white canvas is most pleasant on the eyes and is fun to work in a variety of miniature stitches.
			3 for gros point	18	
		French silk	3 for petit point	22	
7	tan or blue lines on white 36 inches wide	Persian	5 for Tent Stitch	17	
			3 for Cross Stitch (looks and works best)		
5	white 40 inches wide	Paternayan rug wool	1 strand	13	Half Cross Stitch keeps the work less bulky than Tent when stitching a pillow.
4	blue lines on white 40 inches wide	Paternayan rug wool	2 strands for Tent Stitch	13	An excellent canvas for beginners to work with the Cross Stitch. The blue grids help create designs.
			1 strand for Cross Stitch		
		Persian	2 full strands for petit point		
3½	white 40 inches wide	Paternayan rug wool	2 strands for Tent Stitch	13	For those with tired eyes or those in a hurry. Try odds and ends of rug wool in the Long-armed Cross Stitch for a striking rag rug.
			1 strand for Long-armed Cross Stitch (looks and works best)		

Getting Started

Choosing a Design

Nothing could be simpler than a pillow for a first needlepoint project. An average-size pillow, a square of 12 to 18 inches, can contain a simple and interesting design. It involves enough work so that by the time you are through, you will have thoroughly mastered the basic Tent Stitch.

Selecting a first design

A first canvas is a learning piece. It should have an uncomplicated design with about half of the needlepoint area solid background. First master the Tent Stitch worked horizontally and vertically on the design portion and then the diagonal Tent Stitch on the background.

Because you want to concentrate on stitching, select a design with flat areas of color and little shading. Shading is fun and gives life to a design, but you must learn your essentials first. Avoid designs that depend on outlines.

Buying a painted canvas

If you feel all thumbs or if you want to skip all the preliminary steps and get right to it, you may want to invest in a quality hand-painted canvas. It is easy to follow and you can concentrate on the stitches and not on the design. The canvas comes all bound, with proper margins, and with the right amount of wool and the correct size needles. If you work with a reputable shop, you will not only have help in the selection of colors and design, but some personal guidance with the stitching.

A word of caution to the beginner buying a painted canvas: many painted canvases use outlines to separate different areas of color. These lines are not meant to be stitched and are often confusing for a beginner. Stay away from this sort of canvas and look for one that is painted with solid areas of color.

Designing your own

There are many beginners, however, who enjoy figuring everything out for themselves, who enjoy learning from printed instructions, and who will have no trouble learning entirely from this book. If you are one of them, or if you feel ambitious, you can design you own canvas.

Design sources

Sources for designs are very easy to find. Once you become completely involved in canvas work, you will begin to look at everything as a source of inspiration: rugs, vases, lamp bases, fabrics, china and porcelain, and especially the wealth of printed material available—magazines, art books, horticultural and natural history books, children's books, wallpaper, and prints. You can use designs you have found in other needlework areas, such as cross-stitch embroidery, knitting, or crocheting. You can use one of the prepared pillow designs in this book or one of the patterns in the swatches in the Dictionary of Stitches as an all-over repeat.

Custom work

Also possible, but more costly, is taking your ideas to a needlepoint shop and having them design the canvas for you, or if you have a definite design in mind, having them paint it onto the canvas. Many needlepoint shops have very capable artists who can put almost anything on canvas, but the price will be steeper than if you purchased a ready-made design or designed your own. The possibilities for designs are staggering, but whatever you do, you can be sure that your finished piece will be a more personal expression of your tastes and more satisfying than any already stitched item you could possibly buy.

How you go about enlarging or reducing a design taken from a printed source and how you transfer it to your canvas will be covered later in this chapter. How to use repeat patterns is covered on page 44, and instructions for the items in this book accompany their diagrams. For now it is sufficient to know what design you will be using so you can begin collecting your materials and preparing your canvas.

Purchasing and
Preparing the Canvas

Selecting the proper mesh

What mesh canvas you use depends on how simple or intricate your design is, or how important the curving lines are. With more mesh to the inch, you can achieve more detail and greater refinement of shapes. A simple abstract does not call for a petit point canvas. On the other hand, you wouldn't want to work an elaborate picture or a lettered message on too coarse a mesh.

A 10- or 12-mesh mono canvas is a good size for a beginner. The 10 works quickly and looks lovely. However, once you work on a 12-mesh canvas, 10 may seem coarse in comparison. The picture of the Gingham Dog on page 33 is worked on 10-mesh mono, as is the Ribbon Pillow on page 35. The Basket of Flowers Pillow and the Patchwork Pillow (pages 34 and 37) are on 12-mesh mono. The Florentine Pillow (page 36) is on 14.

In deciding how much canvas to purchase for a proposed project, you must determine how large you would like your finished piece to be and then add additional space for seam allowance and margins.

Seam allowance

Allow a few extra rows of needlepoint all around the needlepoint area so that seams can be sewn through needlepoint fabric instead of blank canvas. Three rows are usually sufficient for soft sewn items such as pillows or eyeglass cases. For chair pads, stiffer items, such as handbags, picture frames, wastebaskets, doorstops, or desk accessories, it is a good idea to check with a mounter first. An extra quarter inch of needlepoint all around the work is the usual amount required.

Seam allowance for upholstery

In planning for an upholstery project such as a chair seat, bench, or stool, measure the length, width, and depth of the object and then add to these measurements about 2 inches all around the work for additional rows of needlepoint. This allows the upholsterer sufficient fabric to stretch evenly over the piece and some extra worked fabric to pull and tack in place. Consult an upholsterer before embarking on an ambitious project, and he will make you a paper pattern for your needlepoint area. When purchasing or ordering a hand-painted canvas, specify both the size of the top surface and the size of the drop.

Bare margin allowance

In addition to seam allowance, 1½ to 2 inches of bare canvas should be left all around the worked area. This bare area is for the blocking of the completed work. I usually allow 2 inches all around the canvas just in case I feel the article might look better a little bit bigger or in case the mounter might require a little more allowance.

Preparing the canvas

Canvas is usually sold by the yard or half yard, and you will have to trim it to size. Here is how you do it.
1. Measure the finished size of the work.
2. Add seam allowance to the width and length.
3. Add 2 inches for bare canvas to the width and length.
4. Drag the lead of a pencil between the canvas threads to mark a cutting line.
5. Cut and bind the canvas as described in the next paragraph.
6. Find the center of the bound canvas and mark it lightly with a pencil.
7. Draw a light line around the area to contain the design and a second line to indicate seam allowance.

Binding canvas

Once cut, the canvas is bound on all sides to keep raw edges from fraying. Binding with one-inch masking tape is an easy method and the one which I employ. Apply a half inch to one side, flip the canvas over, and press down the remaining half inch on the other side. A bias tape or cloth tape may be sewn around the edges instead, or the canvas may be hemmed by hand or machine. A machine binding stitch also works well, as do dabs of white glue squeezed along the raw edges.

Direction of canvas

Canvas, like any other fabric, has a direction. When possible, work the needlepoint with the selvedges at the side. It is a good idea to mark the top of the canvas with a "T." This will help the beginner keep all stitches going in the same direction. If the selvedges have been removed, it is still possible to determine which way the mono runs (there is no problem with penelope canvas because the two threads that come closely woven together are the vertical threads). The horizontal thread is flatter and less bumpy than the vertical thread. Take a scrap of canvas and unravel a thread in each direction. The thread that is most crimped is the straight of the goods and should point to the top of the canvas. If you have the misfortune of having to patch a canvas, this information may be of help in matching the patch to the original canvas.

Matching canvases

All pieces of needlepoint to be joined or matched must be worked with the canvas running in the same direction. The number of stitches to the inch from selvedge to selvedge is not the same as the number of stitches along the running yard. Therefore, if two canvases are worked with the canvas running in both directions, they may have an equal number of stitches but unequal dimensions. Case A: Mrs. Z. made a six-piece rug. She stitched four pieces with the canvas held in one direction and two pieces with the canvas held in the other. The result was that the two pieces were longer than the other four. Had she marked each piece with a "T" at the top, she would have avoided the error. Case B: Mrs. Y. made luggage strips from scraps of canvas, using a graph design. One strip finished two inches longer than the other even though the stitch count was identical. She worked the canvases in two different directions.

I have also discovered that some canvases vary from roll to roll, particularly the blue-line rug canvas that is so very easy for beginners to use for the Cross Stitch. Some rolls of this canvas can be 3½ mesh to the inch and others 4 or 4½. Obviously, rug squares or sections on this canvas must come from the same roll. It is therefore wise to purchase at one time enough canvas to complete the project.

Purchasing Yarn

Quantity to purchase

The next thing to figure is how much yarn you need. The price of a painted canvas usually includes sufficient wool to complete the canvas. Persian is generally sold by the ounce in precut strands about 30 inches long. However, when purchasing Persian by the ounce, it is wise to figure out how much you will need totally, and of each color, so you can purchase it all at one time. This is advisable because dye lots can vary, and when using solid areas of color, running out of a shade can create problems. Here is a recipe for estimating the amount of Persian to be worked in Tent Stitching; the same principles may be used for other yarns and stitches.

1. Multiply the number of inches in the length by the number of inches in the width of the area to be worked. In other words, convert the needlepoint area to square inches.
2. Multiply the number of square inches by 1.5: it takes approximately one and a half strands of Persian to Tent Stitch diagonally or horizontally on one square inch of 10-, 12-, or 14-mesh canvas. A test piece might be worked with a strand of any other yarn desired on the particular canvas to be worked. For instance, one strand of heavy rug wool will Tent Stitch one and a half square inches of 5-mesh canvas, so we must now *divide* the total square inches by 1.5 strands.
3. Once we know how many strands are required, it is necessary to convert the strands to ounces. There are about fifty 30-inch strands per ounce of Persian, so we must divide the number of

strands by 50. This gives us the number of ounces for the worked piece.

4. Estimate what percent of the total number of ounces is needed for each color and add an extra ounce to each for any errors in estimating or stitching.

Recipe

If you were trying to estimate the quantity of yarn to purchase for a 14-by-14-inch needlepoint area worked in Tent Stitch on a 10-, 12-, or 14-mesh canvas, the figures would look like this:

> 14 inches × 14 inches = 196 square inches
> 196 square inches × 1.5 strands per inch = 294 strands, rounded off, 300
> 300 strands ÷ 50 strands to an ounce = 6 ounces
> You will need a minimum of 6 ounces.

Florentine Embroidery uses much less yarn. Five ounces is usually sufficient for a 14-by-14-inch pillow.

Color

Do not be afraid to use strong colors in needlepoint. Colors appear more subdued on the canvas because of the shadows cast by the stitches themselves. When in doubt use the stronger value. When trying to achieve the effect of an old piece of needlepoint, you must remember that it has faded greatly. If you get a chance to examine the back of an old piece, you will be amazed at the brightness of the color.

What weight of yarn to use

When in doubt as to how many plies of yarn to use for a particular canvas or for a stitch other than Tent Stitch (for the Tent Stitch see the Canvas Chart on page 8), make a few trial rows in the margin or on a scrap of the same canvas so that you can judge the coverage. The yarn should fill the holes of the canvas and cover the canvas threads without distorting the canvas. A stitch that slants across the mesh uses thinner yarn or fewer plies than a straight stitch, which tends not to cover the canvas threads that run vertically. Although 3-ply Persian is perfect for the Tent Stitch on a 10-mesh canvas, 4-ply is preferable for a straight stitch, the Tent Stitch being diagonal and the straight stitch being vertical. One soon acquires this knowledge instinctively and selects the proper weight.

Length of strands

For wool, a 30-inch strand is a comfortable length to work with. A strand much longer than this is tiresome to pull, and becomes frayed or ragged in stitching. On the other hand, silk or rayon is best worked in strands no longer than 20 inches because in longer lengths they tend to knot and separate.

Cutting a skein

If your wool comes uncut in skeins or bundles, you should cut it in advance for ease in use. Open the skein to a ring. Cut through the ring in one spot when working with short rings. Persian and Nantucket Twist come in long rings and are cut through in two places, at the top and bottom. Loosely knot the bundle of strands in the middle to hold them together.

Storing yarn

Here is a way to keep bundles of yarn tidy that I learned from a customer. Purchase some large loose-leaf notebook rings; they come up to 3 inches in diameter. Fold a bunch of matching strands over a ring and fasten them in two places, below the fold and a few inches from the ends, using twistems or covered wire. To remove a strand, just pluck one from the ring end with one hand, holding the other end with the other hand. A large ring can hold an entire color family.

Storage and work baskets

Work baskets are an attractive addition to almost any room. If the basket is of rough straw, a cotton lining will prevent snagging. A rectangular laundry basket set on a luggage rack is very useful for large projects and convenient to have by your chair. Among storage finds of my own is an old macaroni chest from a grocery store. The glass fronts of the drawers are handsome showcases for neatly stacked yarns and antique pieces of needlepoint. Another real find is a wicker baby's clothes storage hamper on wheels. The individual trays are used to store different colors of yarns and various projects.

Putting a Design on Canvas

To graph or to paint?
There are two ways of transferring a design to a canvas. You may work from a graph or paint the design on the canvas. Graphing is very suitable for geometric designs where counting stitches is involved. It is also an excellent method for designs that are centrally balanced (where a line could be drawn through the middle of the design and one side of it is the reverse of the other). Lettering and repeat patterns may also be worked out on graph paper. However, counting stitches can become tedious. A painted canvas liberates you from the rigid geometry of the graph and facilitates a more natural and free-form design.

Photostats
If you select a design to copy from a book—from these pages or from another printed source—you will probably want to have it enlarged. If you are not an accomplished artist, you can have it done professionally. Take the picture or the book to a shop that specializes in photostats (they are listed in the Yellow Pages) and ask them for a positive stat blown up to the desired size. It will, of course, be enlarged in the same proportions as the original.

Tracing
Once you have your photostat, or an original in the correct size, trace it carefully onto a piece of tracing paper with a black, fine-tipped marking pen. This tracing must be clear enough so that it may be placed under the canvas as a guide. Trace as many of the interior lines as you think will help you keep the form and shape of your design, but don't get bogged down in detail. An absolutely realistic rendering is not necessary. In fact you should try to simplify the design wherever possible. Take a look at the designs for the Gingham Dog and the Basket of Flowers pillow on pages 33 and 34 for an idea of how little detail is necessary. You can always refer to the original if you decide that more detail is necessary later on.

Waterproof mediums only
If you decide to paint the canvas, use a waterproof medium. In most cases blocking and cleaning include a thorough dampening. If the colors are not waterproof, they may very well run and stain the wools. After all the careful work of planning and stitching the canvas, this can be a major disaster.

Oil paints
Oils are a very safe medium. Small tubes of basic colors may be obtained at any art supply store. You will need brushes in at least three different sizes: a very fine one, a medium one, and a larger one for brushing in background. You will also need turpentine for thinning the paint and cleaning the brushes. Because oils take some time to dry and because they are a chore to clean, I prefer using the acrylic paints, which are as readily available.

Acrylics
I have found acrylics to be the clearest, safest, and easiest medium for applying color to canvas. In liquid form, acrylics are water-soluble. This means that colors can be easily thinned and mixed with water, and cleaning paint off brushes and yourself is a simple matter. When the paint is dry, however, it is waterproof. Errors in painting can be "whited out" and corrected. The brand of acrylics we have found to work best is Liquitex.

Mixing cups
You will need some small plastic containers in which to mix your colors. They should have covers to prevent the paint from drying out when not in use. We use one-ounce plastic cups with tops and dab the top of each container with the color contained inside. These containers are washed and reused. If you cannot find them at an art supply store, you can use small plastic pill bottles.

Preparing acrylics
Acrylics come in tubes and jars. Spoon some paint into the container, add water, and stir to the consis-

tency of a light cream. If there is too much water, your canvas will buckle and shrink slightly in the painting. Do not apply the paint too heavily, however, as it will take away from the flexibility of the canvas and make it difficult for the needle to glide through smoothly. A useful gadget to have on hand when using water as a medium is a plastic ketchup-type dispenser for adding drops of water to the paint. To rinse brushes while painting, use two quart-sized jars of water—one for white and light colors, and one for dark colors and black.

Tinting a canvas

You will find acrylics handy to have even if you do not plan to carefully paint in the entire design. I sometimes paint a canvas for Florentine Embroidery in a tint of the main color of the design. Because Florentine Embroidery is composed of straight stitches which tend to leave canvas threads showing, the tinted canvas makes them less apparent. In doing the alphabet letters, which are worked from graphs, we found painting the shadow part of the letters in a dark gray prevented any canvas from showing. It was also pleasanter to stitch without having to count from a graph. If you are planning a simple color scheme for your letters, you might want to tint the body of the letters in the main color to be used.

Brushes for acrylics

You will need brushes for your acrylics. This paint, unfortunately, is not kind to brushes. Nevertheless, decent quality sable brushes are your best investment. You will need a variety of sizes. Start with a few fine and medium sizes.

Magic markers and felt-tipped pens

Many people have had success using these markers. Care must be used in selecting only those which are waterproof. I have never enjoyed working with them, as I find a paint brush more accurate and more pleasant to use. Markers tend to spread their color on the canvas so that a sharp color definition is not easy to achieve. Furthermore, tragedies occur when marker ink runs into the needlepoint during blocking. If you use any of these markers, give them a light spraying with an acrylic fixative before working the canvas.

India ink

Although most India inks are labeled waterproof, they are not generally safe for needlepoint. Black ink is the only India ink that can be made positively waterproof. To make it waterproof, pour the contents of a bottle into a rinsed tin can and set it in a pan of water on the stove. When the water comes to a rapid boil, remove the can and let it cool. Then pour or funnel the ink back into its original bottle. If you are working from a graph and want to do some counting in advance, you can mark off special areas with this ink. It is also helpful for quick outlining and lettering.

Fixative

Waterproof mediums are stressed many times on these pages. A light spraying with an acrylic fixative will seal in any doubts or fears you may have about all of these paints that are supposed to be waterproof. The fixative I have found most successful is called Krylon.

Drawing board

If you plan to paint your own canvases or block the completed work, a good-size piece of half-inch plywood is a worthwhile investment. A piece no smaller than 18 by 20 inches, with sanded edges, can be used on one side for painting and the other side for blocking.

Pushpins

You will need pushpins about 5/8 inch long to tack your canvas over the tracing and into the drawing board so the tracing and canvas don't slip while you are painting. These same tacks are used in blocking.

Eraser

A kneaded rubber eraser purchased at an art supply store is handy for cleaning canvases. It will not leave erasings to get into your yarns as other erasers do. Use it to pick up extra lead from pencil markings that might otherwise stain the yarns.

Painting the canvas

Once you have gathered all your materials, you can begin to paint.

Cover your board with a sheet of white paper. This will not only act as a cushion but it will make your tracing or drawing easier to see. I keep pads of newsprint paper for this purpose. Place the tracing down next and then the canvas. Tack the canvas and the tracing firmly at the top of the board so that the canvas can be lifted if necessary for a closer look at the tracing beneath. Tilt the far end of the drawing board so that it is a few inches higher than the front edge; a pair of bricks will act as a solid prop. A good light also makes it easier to see through the canvas to the design.

Mix the colors to be used. Try to mix the paints into distinct color differences and keep the values of paints much further apart than you plan for them to be in the yarns. The canvas will be easier to paint and simpler to stitch.

Paint from the center out, particularly if there is to be a border around the design. Use as little outline as possible until you are more experienced in painting and in stitching. As you paint, try to think in stitches. For the Tent Stitch, paint on the canvas threads, not in between them, remembering that the stitches are made over the mesh, the point of intersection of a vertical and horizontal canvas thread.

If you have used acrylics or marking pens, the canvas will need practically no drying time. Give the work a light spray of fixative and it is ready for stitching. Oils take longer to dry but require no fixative.

Graphing geometric designs

Geometric designs, repeat patterns, and Florentine Embroidery are easily graphed. Graph paper is generally available in 5, 8, and 10 squares to the inch. Twelve-to-the-inch graph paper can be obtained from architect or drafting suppliers. If your graph paper matches the gauge of your canvas, you can graph your design to scale. This is not essential, however. The important fact to remember is that a square is a stitch even if the scale of the graph is not the same as the canvas. If you are working a 12-inch-wide needlepoint area on a 12-mesh canvas and the only graph paper you can obtain is 10 squares to the inch, multiply the number of canvas stitches to the inch (12) by the width of the work (12). The total, 144, is the number of stitches across the width of the design and the number of boxes you must use on the graph paper.

Graphing nongeometric designs

If your design is not geometric, and you want to put it on graph paper, you must make an adjustment if the canvas and graph paper gauge are not identical. Multiply the number of canvas stitches to the inch by the width of the work. Using the figures used in the preceding example, the total number of stitches required is 144. Divide this total by the size graph paper you are using. If the graph paper has 10 boxes or stitches to the inch, the size of the design should be 14.4 inches. You must enlarge the design to this size for it to be graphed on 10-to-the-inch graph paper and result in 12 inches of needlepoint. You can enlarge it freehand or have it blown up by photostat.

Outlining a design on graph paper

1. Make a careful tracing of the design with a felt-tipped pen.
2. On the tracing, rule a heavy line around the perimeter of the design.
3. On the graph paper, rule a heavy line around the number of squares needed for the design, both in height and width.
4. Place the graph paper over the tracing paper and fasten the two sheets together with pins, staples, or clips.
5. Hold them against a window pane in daylight and trace the design. Use a light box if you have one.

Separate the two pieces of paper and break down the graphed design into colors. Use a pencil so that you can refine the design until it is as close to perfection as possible.

Tent Stitch or cross stitches

When making a graph for a design to be worked in Tent Stitch, consider each box a stitch. For cross stitches, outline as many boxes as each stitch requires. The basic Cross Stitch uses 2 vertical and 2 horizontal canvas threads; this is represented by a square of 4 boxes. Place different symbols in the center of the squares to denote different colors. Key the symbols to what they represent in the margin.

Graphing other stitches   When graphing other stitches, especially fancy stitches or Florentine Embroidery, use the grids of the graph paper as threads of the canvas. Draw the stitches on the graph paper between the vertical grids as they are drawn in the Dictionary of Stitches. In time you will develop your own shorthand methods, perhaps filling in part of the design with these stitch symbols and leaving other sections blank except for the name of the stitch to be worked.

For geometric designs (symmetrical designs that follow a stitch count), graph just a section of the design, enough to solve all the problems that might arise. Lettering should also be planned on graph paper in order to determine how many mesh you will need on the canvas.

Alphabets for Lettering

It is convenient to have a few different styles and sizes of alphabets and number series at your disposal for lettering messages and monograms on pillows, pictures, coasters, and rugs and for initialing or signing your work. On pages 21 and 22 there are four alphabets and two number series.

Lettering may be painted and corrected until perfect on a spare piece of matching canvas; it may be painted directly on the canvas; it may be drawn on a graph first and then painted from the graph; and it may also be stitched directly from a graph.

To plan the layout of a lettered message on canvas, first choose the alphabet you prefer. Count the number of mesh each letter uses, allowing for space between the letters and additional space between words. Now total up the number of mesh to be used in the longest line. Let us say we are going to use this charming bit of advice credited to Lady Mendl:

NEVER COMPLAIN

NEVER EXPLAIN

If we want to do this in the script lettering at the end of the book, using 2 mesh between each letter and 5 mesh between two words, it would work out this way:

$$N \quad E \quad V \quad E \quad R$$
$$11 + 2 + 8 + 2 + 11 + 2 + 8 + 2 + 12 + 5 +$$
$$C \quad O \quad M \quad P \quad L \quad A \quad I \quad N$$
$$8 + 2 + 8 + 2 + 13 + 2 + 9 + 2 + 10 + 2 + 11 + 2 + 8 + 2 + 11$$

The total is 155 mesh for the first line of lettering, not including space on either side for a border or margin. You would not want to work it on too coarse a mesh, as the finished piece would be tremendous. To determine how much space the message will take, you divide the total number of mesh by the number canvas you are interested in working on. If you want to work on a 10-mesh, the number of mesh is divided by ten ($155 \div 10 = 15\frac{1}{2}$).

The message will occupy at least $15\frac{1}{2}$ inches in width. Possibly a 12-mesh would be better: $155 \div 12$ comes to about 13 inches. Allowing for a border, you could make a charming 15-inch-wide pillow. (To see what it would look like on a petit point canvas, see page 1.) The same method must be used to determine the height of the finished piece.

Some artistic judgment should be exercised in determining spacing between letters. Some letters seem to have more "air" around them, such as the J, L, T, and Y, and look better with fewer spaces between them and their neighbors. As you paint or stitch, you can easily make some of these adjustments.

ABCDEFGHIJKL

MNOPQRSTUVW

XYZ&?!

1234567890

ABCDEFGHIJKLMN

OPQRSTUVWXYZ&

ABCDEFGHIJKLMNOPQRS
TUVWXYZ . 1234567890

ABCDEFGH
IJKLMNOPQ
RSTUVWXYZ

ABCDEFGHIJKLMNOPQRS
TUVWXYZ

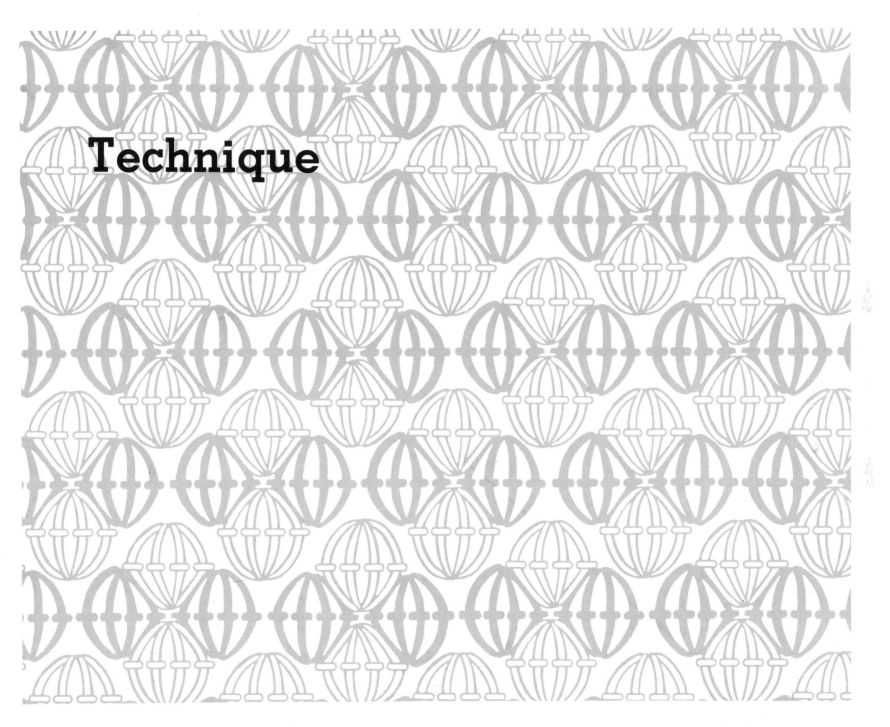

Technique

Working the Canvas

As you work, you will find that the simple mechanics of needlepoint which take such concentration at first will become second nature. Once you catch on, and you will, canvas work will be relaxing and easy. You are sure to find your own ways of doing things, your own special devices and inventions, but to start, here are some hints and preliminary instructions.

Where to begin stitching

Unlike an artist approaching a bare canvas who thinks in large areas, the needlepointer must first think of detail. Once the background is in, it is almost impossible to refine or correct small areas because some of the mesh required has already gone into background, or the stitching has crowded the few mesh necessary and they can barely be seen. The finest details—the veining in a leaf, the center of a flower, the features in a face—are stitched first; then the rest of the design portion is worked. This is especially practical if you plan to use a light background, for the less you handle it the cleaner it will be. When working a large canvas, roll up the edges so you can easily get to the center area.

Some people find backgrounds boring, and working the design and background simultaneously is more pleasant for them. When the background and the design are both to be worked in the diagonal Tent Stitch, it is a good idea to begin stitching in the upper right-hand corner. It is possible to work the diagonal Tent Stitch any place on the canvas if one pays attention to the direction of the canvas threads (see page 49), but it is easier to keep the tension of the stitches even if one row follows the next in an orderly fashion, particularly if there are large areas of solid color.

Direction of yarn

Most yarns, particularly Persian, have a direction. Before threading your needle, hold a strand up to the light and notice that most of the long hairs are going in one direction. Stroke the yarn between your fingers in the direction you think these hairs are going; it should feel smooth. Stroke it in the opposite direction and it will burn the fingers. Put the yarn through the eye of the needle so that these hairs are going away from the needle and consequently away from the canvas. The result will be that the work has a less hairy appearance without losing any of its character. This is a very fine point, and you shouldn't lose sleep over it unless you live in a damp climate where wools can become quite hairy. In this case it is very important.

Folding a single ply

Many needlepointers use a single ply of Persian doubled through the needle. This practice should be discouraged. When the strand is folded in half, the hairs on each half are lying in opposite directions, which makes for fuzzy work.

Threading the needle

To thread your needle, tightly wrap the tail end of the yarn around the sharp edge of the needle eye, pinching the yarn between the thumb and index finger. Keeping the yarn pinched tightly between the fingers so that the sharp fold is not lost, remove the needle and push the eye against the fold. Draw the fold through the eye. This method may take a bit of practice, but it will save much time and effort once it becomes a habit.

Needle threader

When doing petit point and using a very fine needle such as the 22 or 24, I suggest the use of a needle threader. These little wire gadgets can be purchased in a 5-and-10-cent store and are most valuable. The hairpinlike device is easily pushed through the eye of the needle, the wool is slipped through its large opening, then the wire is pulled back through the eye, and the end of the wool along with it.

Threading the needle with silk or cotton

There are times when it is necessary to resort to the most primitive of methods. I have found that the best way to thread a fine needle with silk or cotton is to moisten the end on the tip of your tongue and then flatten the threads to razor sharpness between the

25

thumb and first finger. The end can then slide through the needle's eye.

Anchoring yarn to start

There are many methods of starting. My method is to draw the needle through the mesh opening to the front of the canvas, leaving about one inch of yarn on the back of the canvas. Hold this tail behind the canvas and catch it in the first five or six stitches. In this way you avoid making any knots which might leave lumps on your canvas. Clip away excess yarn.

Anchoring when work is in progress

Starting a new strand once work is in progress is accomplished by sliding or weaving the yarn under five or six stitches on the back of the canvas toward the spot where the needle is to come out in the front.

Ending

End off when the strand with which you have been stitching is about four inches long. Weave the yarn under five or six stitches in the previous row. Clip away the remaining yarn. Start the next strand in the same row as the last few stitches.

Scatter starting and stopping

If possible, try to scatter the starting and ending of yarn. I have seen beginners' work where each row was carefully ended at the end of a row. This causes a ridge along the edge where there is an even area of double threads on the back of the work. If the work is ended in even rows within the work, there will be a line in the work much like the part in one's hair. This is caused by the yarn being pulled evenly to one side when ending and to the other when starting.

Diagonal Tent Stitch: starting and stopping

When starting or ending a strand while working the diagonal Tent Stitch, it is best to weave the new yarn in and out of the basket weave on the wrong side along a horizontal or vertical row. This not only looks better but will help to eliminate a diagonal ridge on the front of the work.

Traveling from one spot to another

When working the same color in neighboring parts of a canvas, I suggest weaving under some stitches on the back of the work to get to the next location. Starting and ending a thread for a few stitches can be a chore and makes lumps on the back of the canvas.

Stitching Tips

Compensating stitches

When doing any stitch that uses more than one mesh, you will find that there are times when there will not be enough canvas threads within the area you are working to complete another full stitch. In such places we use compensating stitches. A compensating stitch is that part of the stitch that will fit in the remaining area. Sometimes these compensating stitches can be anticipated and filled in as you work; other times they may be more easily put in afterward. Sometimes it is best to compensate in advance with a long stitch to avoid too many little compensating stitches. The solutions to these problems become obvious in the course of the work.

An extra stitch

When doing a straight stitch next to a slanting stitch, a bare canvas thread is bound to show. I suggest covering this thread with an extra slanting stitch and sliding it under the neighboring straight stitch.

Back stitch for exposed canvas

The Back Stitch is a very helpful stitch to use when canvas shows. It can be worked between rows of stitches in a thinner strand of the same yarn and in the same color so that it is almost invisible, or it may be purposely worked in another color and perhaps texture as an embellishment. It can be worked over one or two canvas threads. Instructions for the Back Stitch can be found on pages 80–81.

Avoid split ends

When a stitch is made which causes the needle to go into a mesh opening that has already been employed by another stitch, care should be taken so as not to split the yarn already in the opening. Split stitches are not attractive and they make ripping, should it be necessary, very difficult. Push the needle in its own little corner of the mesh opening, and you will have no problem.

A few rules of thumb:
1. Most stitches are begun at the base of the stitch

and go into the canvas at the top of the stitch. This is especially important for Florentine Embroidery and other straight stitches.

2. Most slanting stitches slant at 45-degree angles.
3. When there is more than one slanting stitch to a unit, the stitch that slants from a lower left mesh opening to an upper right is usually on the top or is usually worked last.
4. Work rows of stitches diagonally whenever possible to prevent distortion in the work and to avoid turning the canvas with each row.
5. When stitches are made to travel diagonally across the canvas, from an upper left corner to a lower right corner and then back again from right to left, the areas that did not get worked can be done with the canvas turned upside down, starting from the upper right corner.
6. To reverse the direction of a stitch (to make a stitch slant in the opposite direction), give the canvas a quarter turn, so that the top of the canvas is now at the side, and continue stitching as before.

Twisting   Yarn tends to twist as you work. With each stitch give the needle a slight turn in the opposite direction of the twist. After a while you will do this automatically. If it is easier, however, a novice can simply let the needle dangle and the yarn will straighten itself.

Since the canvas is held with one hand and the stitching is done with the other, it is very comfortable to hold the yarn close to the last stitch with the thumb of the canvas hand, keeping the threads aligned and flat. Release the yarn just before completing the new stitch, and the yarn will flip over in place without twisting.

Fuzziness   Sometimes a long-haired yarn such as Persian seems unusually hairy, so much so that when worked it almost seems to have a beard. Dampness in the air or much handling may be the cause. Follow the advice under Direction of Yarn to avoid having these hairs stand on end.

Shading and Blending

There are many ways of using colors on your canvas. For bold abstracts, geometrics, repeats, Florentine Embroidery, and very contemporary pictures, you can use flat, unmodulated areas of color. For period pieces, primitives, and realistic renderings, a feeling of depth or roundness is desired.

Shading   This illusion of three-dimensionality is accomplished through subtle shading. Select the main colors and a few closely related values for each. Use the lighter values to illuminate areas of the form that project and which in nature would catch light. Use the darker values for areas that are recessed or which would be cast in shadow. Lighter values are usually used in the center, darker values toward the edges. If you are copying from a color picture, you can follow the gradations of the picture itself: notice which areas of the picture are lighter and which are darker and use different values accordingly. Do not stop each value abruptly in straight lines, but instead stagger the rows so that the changes in tone are almost imperceptible.

Shadows   A shadow cast onto the background also has the effect of rendering an object in depth and making it look realistic. If you do not know where to put a shadow behind an object, find an object similar in shape, place it on a flat surface, and shine a light down on it from various angles. You will then see where a shadow can be cast, at what angle, and how to be consistent in shadowing other objects in the composition.

You can use these devices to whatever extent you wish, but I suggest that a beginner make her first piece without much modeling. It is easier to learn needlepoint without these distractions. Once you have mastered the preliminaries of stitching, you will have a good deal of fun with modeling.

Blending is a useful method of shading when close values are desired. I have used it with many different stitches throughout this book (see the letters E, G, J, Q, U, and W of the Alphabet Sampler).

FOR 3-PLY WOOL	FOR 2-PLY WOOL
3-ply color A	2-ply color A
2-ply color A + 1-ply color B	1-ply color A + 1-ply color B
1-ply color A + 2-ply color B	2-ply color B
3-ply color B	1-ply color B + 1-ply color C
2-ply color B + 1-ply color C	2-ply color C
1-ply color B + 2-ply color C	Etc.
3-ply color C	
Etc.	

Using a 2-ply wool, the blending moves along much quicker. On a background you might want to subtly return to the first value. The effect is very much like a lovely hand-dyed wool in an Oriental or Persian carpet.

The number of rows to each value must be judged according to the design. It can be done so that there is only one lightening and darkening or many. Or each time a needleful is completed, the value can be changed. In this case a striated effect is achieved.

When subtle blending is desired, try using any of the stitches that interlock, one row into the next, such as the Brick Stitch, Back Stitch, Encroaching Gobelin Stitch, Kalem Stitch, Parisian Stitch, and Hungarian Stitch.

Blending diagonal Tent Stitch

If you are using a diagonal Tent Stitch and wish to blend your colors for a horizontal effect, you must stagger the length of your diagonal rows. First mark the canvas margins into the number of value changes desired. Stitch diagonally but stagger the length of the rows so that the right edge of the worked area is very ragged. When you come to your value change, fill in the skipped mesh with the next value and continue stitching diagonally, likewise staggering each row.

Repairs

While a canvas is in progress and a correction can be made, I am definitely in favor of making it. The satisfaction gained from regarding your own work with approval completely overshadows the tedium of ripping, so when in doubt—rip!

Most errors show themselves pretty fast. Each time you pick up your work you should scan it briefly. When working stitches other than the Tent Stitch, errors usually show themselves in the next row of stitches, as the stitch count is upset.

Top and side

The most common error beginners make is accidentally changing the direction of their stitches by turning their canvas so that the top is at the side. Mark the top of the canvas with a "T" and keep the "T" on top or bottom. If you give the canvas a quarter turn in either direction—so the "T" is on the side—you will automatically reverse the slant of your stitches. If you were working a Tent Stitch, it would now slant from lower right to upper left instead of lower left to upper right. There will be times when you will want to reverse the direction of your stitches, but don't do it accidentally.

Missed stitches

If you miss a stitch, it is of little concern. I often tell beginners not to make a stitch if they are not convinced it is needed. It is very easy to slip in extra stitches later. After the canvas is completed, hold it up to the light; light will sparkle through the empty spots in the mesh.

Ripping

When you have to rip a stitch or two, don't try to "unstitch" them—you will weave a very tangled web. It is much more efficient to unthread the needle and lift out the stitches with the blunt end of the needle.

To rip out a section of your work, a pair of fine-pointed embroidery scissors should be employed. Carefully slip the blade under the stitches on the front of the canvas. Lift them up and away from the canvas to avoid cutting the canvas itself, and clip as many as you can at one time. Then turn the canvas to the wrong side, fluff up the stitches with the needle, and brush away all the bits of yarn. I find fluffing away the bits on the back of the canvas keeps the front of the work cleaner. Repeat this process until you have eliminated the error. Then, using the end of your needle, undo stitches on both sides of the incision until you have enough yarn to thread into the needle. Weave both ends into the back of the work. If you do not have enough yarn to comfortably thread the needle or if you do not feel like undoing a few more inches of work to acquire the extra yarn, weave the unthreaded needle under five or six stitches on the back of the canvas where you plan to end off. Thread it in this position and draw it through.

With every canvas that you work, an improvement in technique and in artistic quality will be obvious. As a matter of fact, most people find when they are half through with the work that they are so much more skillful they wish they could rip it out and start over. Don't. Keep going. Every piece will be better than the last, and that's half the fun of it. After even the most primitive work is blocked and mounted, it will look good; so enjoy learning and date your work, then the improvement shown will be an added attraction. By the time a canvas is completed, only minor corrections should be made, filling in missed stitches or cleaning up the back of the canvas.

Patching

When ripping some stitches, you may accidentally cut one of the canvas threads. The canvas can be easily "darned" in the following manner.

1. Cut a 3-inch square of the same mesh-count canvas and center it behind the damaged portion. Be sure the patching piece of canvas is being held in the same direction as the ripped piece (see Direction of Canvas, page 15). Line up the horizontal and vertical canvas threads.

2. Needlepoint through both pieces of canvas in an area of about a square inch.

3. Clip away extra spare canvas on the back.

Restoration

After a great deal of handling, even the best of canvases will become limp. A steam ironing will reactivate the starch and bring the canvas back to its original body. After blocking a completed piece of needlepoint, some additional rows may be needed. Sufficient starch may still be left in the canvas to be reactivated by another steam ironing. If not, carefully cover the needlepoint and spray the bare canvas with starch.

Finishing Touches

Blocking

After the completion of a canvas, the work requires a blocking to straighten the canvas and to flatten the stitches for a smooth texture. This can sometimes be accomplished by a good steaming with a steam iron on the wrong side of the canvas. When a piece of work is badly distorted, it should be dampened or even soaked and nailed face down to dry. A very badly misshapen canvas (one surely not done in a diagonal Tent Stitch) will sometimes need two or three blockings. There should be no need for this much blocking once proper stitch technique is mastered.

To block your own piece, you will need:
A large turkish towel
Clean brown wrapping paper
A board one-half inch thick and larger than your canvas
Tacks
A T-square, ruler, or right angle

1. Soak the towel in cold water and wring it well.
2. Tightly roll the canvas in the towel.
3. Place the wrapping paper on the board.
4. Tack the needlepoint to the board, face down. Be sure you put the tacks about an inch away from the work so that tack marks or rust will not appear on it. Start by tacking across one

side, then pull it in shape and tack the other side while pulling. Do the other two sides in the same fashion. Test the straightness of the canvas with the T-square.

5. Allow the canvas to dry thoroughly—for at least 24 hours—before removing it from the board.

Washing before blocking

Sometimes completed needlepoint canvases need to be washed before they are mounted. Use Woolite and cold water, following the directions on the box.

Mounting

I feel that people who really love to needlepoint are usually not the great seamstresses of the world, and that most of their items should be mounted professionally.

Pillows can be made by an upholsterer. If you have just completed your first or second canvas, take it to a local upholsterer who will block it and make it into an acceptable pillow at a modest price. However, when it is a work of art, and surely it will be, inquire about mounting at your needlepoint store. They usually have people who can mount various items with great skill. Decorators also have favorite workrooms where they have such things made. Pillows, rugs, chair seats, and upholstery go to one type of shop. Hard goods such as address-book covers, telephone books, and wastebaskets go to a shop where leather goods are made. Pictures go to a frame shop. Slippers are made by very fine shoemakers and are costly to have mounted. A good tailor will make a vest, but consult him about the pattern before you start. He will draw a pattern for you so that he will have enough needlepoint fabric. Allow extra canvas all around the worked area in case more needlepoint is necessary later.

You may find mounting a small rug, a hanging, or a belt easy to do by yourself. After blocking, sharply press the raw edges to the wrong side and tack them in place. A rug should be lined with a heavy fabric that will wear well, such as an upholsterer's linen. A hanging or a belt should be lined with lighter material such as felt or moiré; ribbon is excellent for a belt. Cut the fabric about $5/8$ inch larger than the completed needlepoint. Press the $5/8$ inch to the wrong side of the fabric. Hand tack it to the back of the needlepoint.

Washing mounted needlepoint

After needlepoint pillows or upholstery have been around for some time, they may require cleaning. Mix a basin of Woolite and cold water. With a sponge, scoop up some foam and draw it gently across the needlepoint. Wring the sponge in cold water and draw it across the needlepoint again to rinse.

Pillows and Other Things to Make

Chessboard

The Chessboard on page 1 of photo insert is designed to hang on the wall when not in use. The Chessboard is composed of diagonal repeats, also worked in 2-ply Persian. Starting at the upper right: Hungarian Ground Stitch, Scottish Stitch, Hungarian Stitch, Jacquard Stitch, Byzantine Stitch, and Parisian Stitch worked on its side. Monograms are on Tent Stitch. The border uses 3-ply Persian in rows of Straight Gobelin of varying widths. One-ply Persian is used for the Back Stitch which is set in last between the rows. Note corners of the Gobelin border are mitered.

Gingham Dog

This is not only an easy canvas for a beginner to paint but it also serves as a simple introduction to a number of basic stitches. The 14-by-14-inch design can be made into a pillow as well as a picture. Enlarge it freehand or by photostat. Allow three rows for seam allowance in addition to margins if you are making a pillow. Three-ply Persian is used on a 10-mesh mono canvas. Section A is worked in Large Chequer Stitch, B in Cashmere Stitch, and C in Mosaic Stitch. Everything else is worked in Tent Stitch except for the eyes which are Straight Gobelin (an underlay of horizontal stitches is put in first for padding).

Basket of Flowers

This pillow (or picture) is a little more advanced than the Gingham Dog. The stitches are more difficult and some shading in the flowers is required. It measures 14 by 14 inches and is worked on a 12-mesh mono canvas. Enlarge the design by photostat or freehand. Trace the enlargement and draw in the shading from the photograph. Then paint the whole design onto the canvas. Section A is worked in Brick Stitch, B in Encroaching Gobelin, and C in Scottish Stitch. Surrey Stitch is used for fringe which is stitched before blocking. The two shades of green used in the leaves are also used for the fringe. Two shades of gold are used for shading the basket. The Brick Stitch is worked in 3-ply Persian; the ribbon and flower centers in rayon; everything else is 2-ply Persian.

Persian Vest

The design motifs in the Persian Vest come from a book on Oriental rugs. One half of the canvas is painted and then the design is painted in reverse on the other side. The stitches, too, are reversed so that most stitches slant toward the center. The stitches used for accent are Mosaic, Continuous Mosaic, and Slanting Gobelin. The major part of the vest is worked in Tent Stitch with 2-ply Persian on a 12-mesh mono canvas.

Ribbon Pillow

The needlepoint surface on this pillow measures 15 by 15 inches. Three-ply Persian is used on a 10-mesh mono canvas. The design can be penciled or painted onto the canvas from the photograph. Locate the center of the canvas and mark it. Locate the center of the third vertical ribbon (ribbons are 12 canvas threads wide by 28 canvas threads long). Count up 14 horizontal canvas threads and start painting the center band of ribbon.

To stitch, work horizontal ribbons first with the top of the canvas at the top. To work the vertical ribbons, turn the canvas so that the top is at the side. The center of the ribbon is a Flat Stitch over 4 horizontal by 4 vertical canvas threads. It is outlined by two rows of horizontal Tent Stitch and one row of Slanting Gobelin over 2 canvas threads. (A swatch of the ribbon is worked as an example of the Flat Stitch on page 65.) To work the curved ends of the ribbons use the Tent Stitch following the direction of the stitches in that row of ribbon.

The entire background, including shadows, is worked in Tent Stitch. Do the background after the ribbons are put in. The bands will appear to wave giving them a ribbonlike look. Bumps that occur in the squares of background between the bands of ribbon will flatten in blocking. However, the waving of the ribbon should not be straightened in the blocking.

Top for horizontal ribbons (white)

Top for vertical ribbons (black)

35

Florentine Pillow

The five patterns on this little 8 by 10 inch pillow are Florentine Embroidery and they are all worked by counting. The pillow can be enlarged by adding more rows of straight stitches or more sections. A 14-mesh mono canvas is used with 3-ply Persian wool. Tint the canvas in a medium value of the main color to avoid noticeable grin-through.

A. Wave Stitch with Hungarian Stitch and Hungarian Diamond fillings; 4.1 step and 2.1 step.
B. Florentine Stitch in blocks of 4 stitches at the base, rising and falling 4 stitches in flames; 4.2 step.
C. Hungarian Ground; a pattern often used with Florentine Stitches.
D. Rounded waves; 4.1 step and 3.1 step.
E. Bargello; diamonds are over 2, 4, 6 threads at intersections; 3.1 step. The diamond fillings are worked in 2 colors. Stitches are taken dividing the diamonds in halves and quarters.

A canvas can be divided diagonally into large and small diamonds and each section worked in a different Florentine Embroidery stitch.

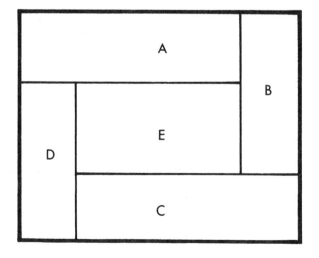

A simple checkerboard design divides a canvas into even squares that can be filled with a variety of stitches.

Patchwork Pillow

Making a patchwork pillow is a fine way to use the many stitches in this book. Because this pillow is geometric in design it can be cut off at any point for a smaller pillow or added on to for a larger piece of work. The design is easy to enlarge. All lines are straight lines and all angles either 45 or 90 degrees. Start painting the canvas from the center out. Even though the design is round (16½ inches in diameter) it is worked on a square piece of canvas. The canvas is 12-mesh mono; 2-ply Persian is used for slanting stitches and 3-ply for straight stitches.

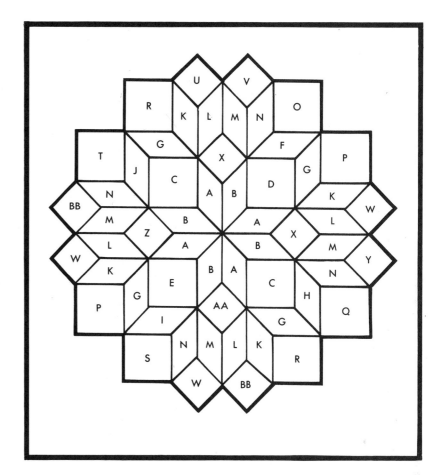

A. Slanting Gobelin Stitch
B. Jacquard Stitch
C. Leaf Stitch
   Mosaic Stitch
   Tent Stitch
D. Eyelet Stitch
   Mosaic Stitch
   Tent Stitch
E. Diamond Eyelet Stitch
   Mosaic Stitch
   Tent Stitch
F. Parisian Stitch
G. Oriental Stitch
H. Scottish Stitch
I. Hungarian Stitch
J. Continuous Flat Stitch
K. Mosaic Stitch
L. Continuous Mosaic Stitch
M. Milanese Stitch
N. Wave Stitch
O. Tied Cross Stitch
P. Leviathan Stitch
   Back Stitch

Q. Shell Stitch
R. Cushion Stitch
   Tent Stitch
S. Shell Stitch
T. Large and Straight Cross
   Stitch (the large cross is
   tied down)
U. Wave Stitch
V. Wave Stitch
   Tent Stitch
W. Wave Stitch
   Hungarian Stitch
X. Jacquard Stitch
Y. Slanting Gobelin Stitch
   Eyelet Stitch
   Tent Stitch
Z. Leviathan Stitch
   Smyrna Stitch
   Tent Stitch
AA. Triangle Stitch
   Tent Stitch
BB. Large Chequer Stitch
Background. Tent Stitch

My Vest

Outline the shape of the vest on the canvas to establish the needle-point area. Place the design motifs on the vest so that there are complete repeats across each half of the vest. These motifs may be outlined first in pencil. Paint the Flat Stitches only (they are the boxlike stitches that make up the major design motif). It is not necessary to paint the filling stitches.

Work the Flat Stitches first, blending the yarns. More blending is achieved by using half lengths of the wool strands. Then fill in the areas as indicated on the chart with Byzantine Stitch, Jacquard Stitch, and Cushion Stitch surrounded with Tent Stitch. Work the border in Jacquard Stitch using random colors. All of these stitches are in 2-ply Persian. Put the background in last using a Back Stitch of French linen. Be careful to keep these Back Stitches flat by not letting the linen become twisted and by not splitting stitches in the work. A tan 11/22-mesh penelope canvas was used but a 10/20 canvas may be substituted if not obtainable. Be sure that the canvas is tan if, as in My Vest, a tan linen thread is used.

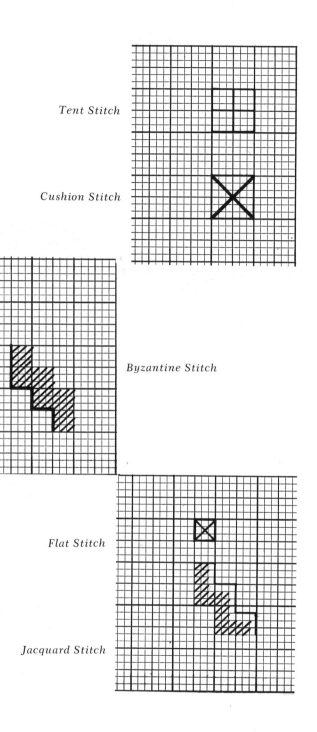

Tent Stitch

Cushion Stitch

Byzantine Stitch

Flat Stitch

Jacquard Stitch

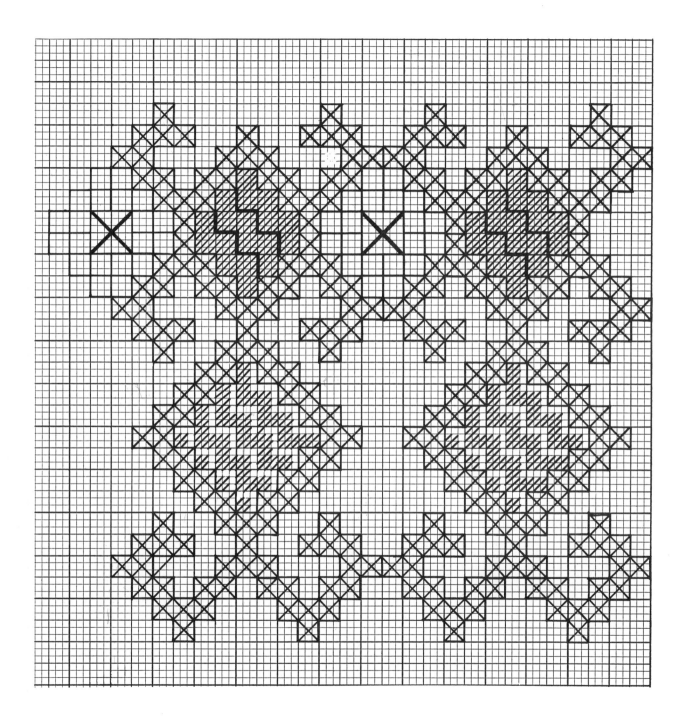

Dictionary of Stitches

Dictionary Guide

Needlepoint is more than a single canvas stitch. It encompasses a wide variety of stitches, some so decorative, with so much texture and pattern, that just the repeated stitch creates a handsome design.

Two basic stitches

There are two basic stitches, a slanting stitch and a straight stitch. Most people are familiar with the slanting stitch; it is called Tent Stitch, Continental Stitch, or petit point. The straight stitch is the Gobelin Stitch. These two stitches are the foundation of all the others. Embellishments are added, one after another, and with each new addition or variation the stitch is given a new name.

Four sections

The Dictionary of Stitches is divided into four sections: Slanting Stitches, Straight Stitches, Cross Stitches, and Tied and Looped Stitches. The Cross Stitches and Tied and Looped Stitches are combinations of the two basic stitches. The easiest stitches in each category are placed first, then the embellishments and variations follow in logical progression.

Instructions

The instructions for each stitch embody the methods I have found most efficient. They prevent yarn from slipping through the threads of mono canvas, keep stitching comfortable, and eliminate odd positions of the hands and canvas. Most important, they assure beautiful stitches and even work. Rules, however, are made to be broken, so try these stitches as shown but also experiment and incorporate your own methods.

Numbering system

The numbering system used on the diagrams is simple. Unless specifically noted, the needle is brought up through the mesh opening from the back of the work at 1, and then down through the next mesh opening at 2. 1 is up and 2 is down. It follows that all odd numbers come up through the canvas and even numbers go down through the canvas. Additional instructions have been supplied for those to whom stitching does not come easily. "Naturals" or old hands at needlepoint will find the diagrams alone sufficient. In the instructions they will also find some tips for better stitching and some suggestions for stitch use.

Right-handed and left-handed

The diagrams are designed for right-handed people. If you are left-handed these same diagrams can be followed by simply turning the book upside down. A right-handed person starts most stitches at the base of the stitch; a left-handed person starts at the top of the stitch. This eliminates uncomfortable maneuvering without altering the careful stitch formation.

Maxi and mini stitches

Most of the diagrams and swatches are shown on mono canvas because I feel the stitches are easier to master on this single-threaded canvas. However, some stitches look more interesting worked in miniature, using the individual threads of penelope canvas; others can be worked in maximum size on rug canvases. Experiment with both mini and maxi stitches.

Using the Stitches and Swatches

Using interesting background stitches

Too much background is the constant complaint of the avid needlepointer. However, many designs need a quiet area around them. The way to avoid the tedium of a large area of solid Tent Stitch is to use some of the quieter, small-scale stiches such as Reversed Tent, Reversed Half Cross (on penelope only), Rep Stitch, Kalem, Mosaic, Continuous Mosaic, Small Chequer, Scottish, Brick, Back, Parisian, Hungarian, Cross, Upright Cross, Long-armed Cross, and Greek Stitch.

Using stitches to simulate reality

Take full advantage of the many stitches. In pictorial designs, use stitches that simulate the actual texture of what is being represented. Use feathery stitches or rugged stitches when the subject matter calls for it. A quiet Brick Stitch is perfect for a calm, peaceful sky, shaded so that the darkest value appears to be further away, on the horizon, and the lightest area overhead, or at the top of the picture. Many of the stitches have usage suggestions noted along with the instructions. See the Genesis Sampler on pages 2–3 of photo insert for other ideas of how stitches can be used for their texture. Once these stitches are part of your needlepoint vocabulary you will find many uses for them. They are stimulating to use and your work will be greatly admired.

Using the swatches

The swatches that accompany the stitch instructions are intended to be a source of inspiration and a reference guide for making stitch selections. Many of them have also been worked in designs that can be used to make pillows, belts, purses, and upholstery.

The stitch itself

In some cases, one stitch alone can be used for an entire piece. If the stitch has sufficient pattern just the use of color is needed to create design. The stitch can be used as is, or it can be worked in various directions or used with variations of itself. Look at the swatches of the Leaf, Continuous Mosaic, Moorish, Byzantine, Jacquard, Milanese, Oriental, Knotted, and Shell stitches. Each could be used as fabric for a variety of needlepoint pieces.

Combined stitches

In other swatches, several stitches are combined to create designs. Cashmere Stitch and Continuous Cashmere Stitch; Continuous Flat Stitch and Mosaic Stitch; Algerian Eye Stitch and Flat Stitch; Straight Gobelin Stitch and Smyrna Stitch; Wave Stitch with Diamonds; and Triangle Stitch and Mosaic Stitch. The first stitch listed is the swatch on which the two stitches appear.

Enlarging swatches

The designs in other swatches can be enlarged by increasing the number of rows for each color or stitch. The Large Chequer, Small Chequer, Leviathan and Smyrna, Triangle and Hungarian Stitch swatches are good selections for enlargement.

Repeat patterns

Another way of using the swatches is in repeat patterns. The design motif in the swatch is repeated over and over again in a systematic order. There are four different kinds of repeats.

1. A repeat can be made directly above, beneath, and on both sides of the motif.
2. A repeat can be staggered in brick fashion in horizontal rows. Motifs in one row are side by side but in alternate rows the motifs are centered between those in the row above.
3. A repeat can be staggered on the side. Motifs in one vertical row are directly under one another but in alternate vertical rows the motifs are centered between those in the rows to the left and right. This is called Half-drop Repeat.
4. The motif can also be reversed on all four sides when it is repeated. This is called a Mirror Repeat. You can actually place a mirror perpendicular to a design to see how it will look reversed.

Some of the swatches that would make choice repeats are the Triple Cross, Rococo, Mosaic, Diamond Eyelet, Slanting Gobelin, Flat Stitch, and Flame Stitch carnation swatches.

Patchwork

One last suggestion for the swatches is to use them for a patchwork. Stitch the different squares next to one another in checkerboard fashion on the same canvas.

Slanting Stitches

Tent Stitch
Half Cross Stitch
Reversed Half Cross Stitch
Tramé
Reversed Tent Stitch
Rep Stitch
Slanting Gobelin Stitch
Kalem Stitch
Encroaching Gobelin Stitch
Stem Stitch
Leaf Stitch
Mosaic Stitch
Continuous Mosaic Stitch
Small Chequer Stitch
Cashmere Stitch
Continuous Cashmere Stitch
Flat Stitch
Cushion Stitch
Large Chequer Stitch
Scottish Stitch
Continuous Flat Stitch
Moorish Stitch
Byzantine Stitch
Jacquard Stitch
Milanese Stitch
Oriental Stitch
Algerian Eye Stitch
Eyelet Stitch
Diamond Eyelet Stitch

This partly stitched 24-mesh mono canvas is worked in Tent Stitch. The petit point background is worked diagonally, and the flower horizontally, vertically, and diagonally. The flower is done in 3-ply French silk. Notice how the texture differs from the background which is worked in 1-ply Nantucket Twist. This is an example of a good hand-painted canvas.

Tent Stitch

Also called Continental Stitch and Petit Point

Tent Stitch is the bread-and-butter stitch. It is the most used and most adaptable needlepoint stitch and is often used to the exclusion of all others for an entire canvas. It is used in just about every swatch in this section of the book, and in the Alphabet Sampler where it is used to outline all the letters.

Tent is the smallest needlepoint stitch; it covers only one mesh whereas almost all other stitches cross at least two. The stitch slants from lower left to upper right, crossing the intersection of a vertical and horizontal canvas thread (diagram 1). There are three ways in which it can be worked: horizontally (2), vertically (3), and diagonally (4).

Horizontal Tent should be used primarily where a single row of horizontal stitches is required. It should not be used to work large areas because it will pull the canvas badly out of shape. Rows of horizontal Tent are always worked from right to left, each stitch taken directly beside the last (5). Draw needle out from underside to front of canvas at 1, go in 2, out 3, in 4, and so on.

When using this stitch in a small area of more than one row, the work must be turned upside down at the end of each row in order to keep stitching from right to left (6 & 7).

Row 1. Start with top line of work; stitch from right to left.

Row 2. Turn work so that top of canvas becomes bottom. Draw needle out 1, in 2, out 3, and so on.

Row 3. Turn work so that top of canvas is at top. Draw needle out 1, in 2.

If there are only 1, 2, or 3 stitches in the rows directly beneath the one you have just completed, do not bother to turn the canvas, but continue on to the next row, working from right to left.

Vertical Tent should be used primarily where a single row of vertical stitches is required. Each stitch is taken directly beneath the last, working from top to bottom. The canvas is turned on completion of each row (8). Draw needle out from underside to front of canvas at 1, in 2, out 3, in 4, and so on.

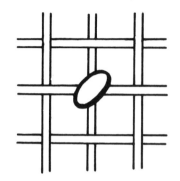

1. Tent Stitch.

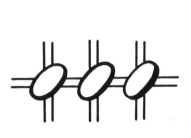

2. Horizontal Tent Stitch.

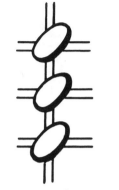

3. Vertical Tent Stitch.

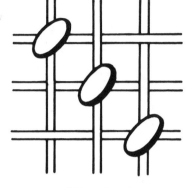

4. Diagonal Tent Stitch.

5. Single row of horizontal Tent Stitch.

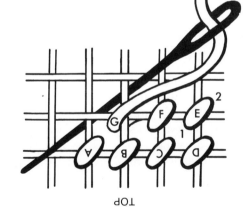

6. Canvas is in this position for Row 2.

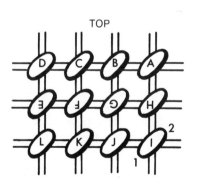

7. Canvas is in this position for Row 3.

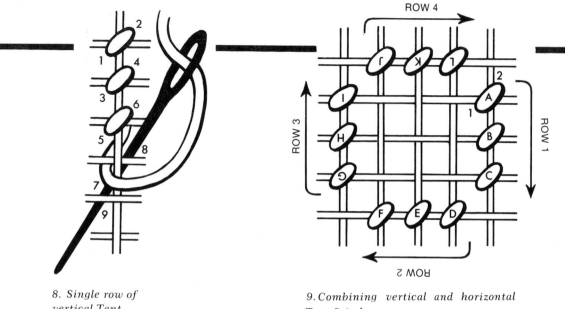

8. *Single row of vertical Tent Stitch.*

9. *Combining vertical and horizontal Tent Stitch.*

Vertical Tent is often combined with horizontal Tent for outlining and veining. Work from top down and from right to left (9).

Row 1. Start vertical row with A; draw needle out 1, in 2.

Row 2. Start horizontal row with D; work from right to left.

Row 3. Turn canvas upside down; start vertical row with G.

Row 4. Start horizontal row with J; work from right to left.

The preferred and most successful way of working Tent Stitch is diagonally. For a beginner it is a little more difficult than the horizontal Tent but it is well worth the time spent learning it. Worked diagonally, it causes little distortion and can be used for backgrounds and large areas of work. A slight variation in the slant of each diagonal row gives it a very pleasing textured effect whereas the horizontal Tent, at its best, has a ridged appearance and, at its worst, looks lumpy. On the back of the canvas emerges an equally pleasing basketweave pattern (10). And not least among its advantages is you need not turn the canvas with each row.

Diagonal Tent is worked across the canvas in ascending and descending rows (11), changing colors as necessary. It is customarily started in a right-hand corner but it can be started anyplace on the canvas. Descending rows should be worked over those diagonal rows of canvas threads that have a vertical thread on top (12) and the ascending rows over those that have a horizontal thread on top (13). If the alternation of ascending and descending rows is followed closely, you will never lose the basketry on the back of the canvas, your colors will mesh neatly one into the other, and you can work any place on the canvas secure in the knowledge that the basketweave will join in the end and you will have a beautiful unridged piece of needlepoint.

Starting from the upper right-hand corner of the work:

Row 1. Draw needle out 1, in 2. Because a vertical canvas thread is on top, we know that this next row is a descending row. Draw needle out 3, in 4, out 5, in 6; end of first descending row (14).

Row 2. Draw needle out 7, in 8, out 9, in 10, out 11, in 12; end of first ascending row (15).

Row 3. Draw needle out 13, in 14, out 15, in 16, and so on, ending with in 20; end of second descending row (16).

To start diagonal Tent in an interior section of the canvas you have to locate a first row of stitches. If the diagonal row on which you choose to begin has a vertical thread on top it should be worked from top to bottom (descending). If a horizontal canvas thread is on top, your first row should be worked from bottom to top (ascending). The first row can be made with as few as two stitches.

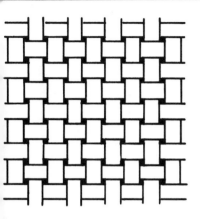

10. Back of canvas worked in diagonal Tent Stitch creates a "basketweave."

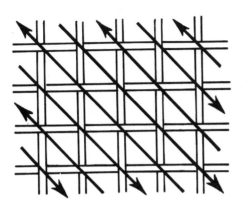

11. Arrows indicate direction of diagonal rows.

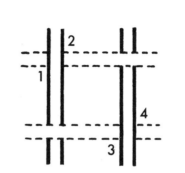

12. Vertical canvas thread on top; a descending row. Out 1, in 2.

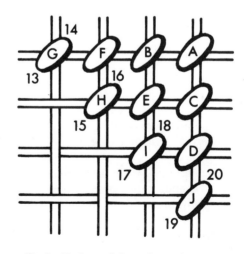

13. Horizontal canvas thread on top; an ascending row. Out 1, in 2.

With your fingernail, trace along a diagonal row of mesh. Notice that one row has a vertical thread on top of a horizontal and the next a horizontal thread on top of a vertical. Work diagonal rows with a vertical thread on top as descending rows; work those rows with a horizontal thread on top as ascending rows. I thank and credit Maggie Lane for this valuable tip.

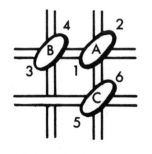

14. Starting in a corner; B and C make a descending row because the vertical canvas thread in on top.

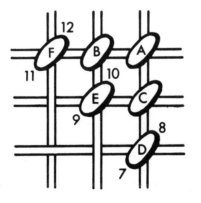

15. D, E, and F make an ascending row because the horizontal canvas thread is on top.

16. G, H, I, and J make a descending row.

49

Tent Stitch

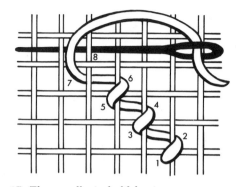

17. *The needle is held horizontally and goes under 2 vertical canvas threads. Notice ascending row is traveling on canvas threads that have a horizontal thread on top.*

Ascending row (17)

1. Out 1, lower left hole of first stitch.
2. In 2, upper right hole of first stitch; needle is held in a horizontal position and goes under two vertical canvas threads.
3. Out 3, the lower left of the next stitch in the diagonal row.
4. In 4; needle is held in a horizontal position and goes under two canvas threads.
5. Out 5, in 6, and so on.

Descending row (18)

1. Out 1, the lower left hole of first stitch.
2. In 2, the upper right hole of first stitch; needle is now held in a vertical position and goes under two horizontal canvas threads.
3. Out 3, the lower left hole of the next stitch in the diagonal row.
4. In 4, out 5, and so on.

Notice that ascending rows make horizontal lines on the back of the canvas and descending rows make vertical lines. If you are ever confused upon resuming work about which direction to work your diagonal row, examine the back of the canvas. If the last few stitches are horizontal you were coming up the row; if the last few stitches are vertical you were going down the row. The direction of the canvas threads will also give you the same information.

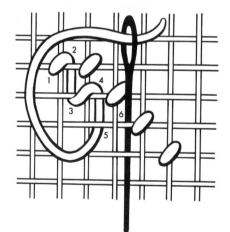

18. *The needle is held vertically and goes under 2 horizontal canvas threads. Notice descending row is traveling on canvas threads that have a vertical thread on top.*

Half Cross Stitch

Also called Half Stitch

The Half Cross Stitch, like the Tent Stitch, is one of the basic small stitches. It is worked only on penelope canvas because it would slide through the threads of mono canvas and look uneven.

Unlike the Tent Stitch, in which there is as much wool on the back of the canvas as there is on the front, the Half Cross leaves a minimum of wool on the back. It is very economical of yarn and produces a thin flat piece of work which makes it particularly useful for heavy wools. Try it with rug wool on 5-mesh penelope. Handsome pillows and pictures may also be worked in this stitch, thereby eliminating the additional bulk of the Tent Stitch.

The Half Cross Stitch can be worked both vertically and horizontally though it is, in fact, prettier worked vertically. Worked vertically, the stitch shapes itself more clearly, coming almost to a point at the top like the Tent Stitch. Worked horizontally, the stitch is flatter, not as sharply defined.

The horizontal Half Cross is worked across the canvas from left to right. The canvas must be turned after each row to continue working left to right.

Row 1. Draw needle out from underside to front of canvas at 1, in 2, out 3, and so on. The needle is held in a vertical position; it goes in a top hole and comes out directly beneath it (19).

Row 2. Turn the canvas so the top is at the bottom and continue stitching left to right (20). At the end of the row, the canvas is turned rightside up again.

The vertical Half Cross is worked from the bottom up. At the end of each row the canvas must be turned.

Row 1. Draw needle out 1, in 2, out 3. The needle is held in a horizontal position; it goes in the hole to the right of the double threads and comes out directly beside them (21).

Row 2. Turn the canvas rightside up and continue stitching from the bottom up (22).

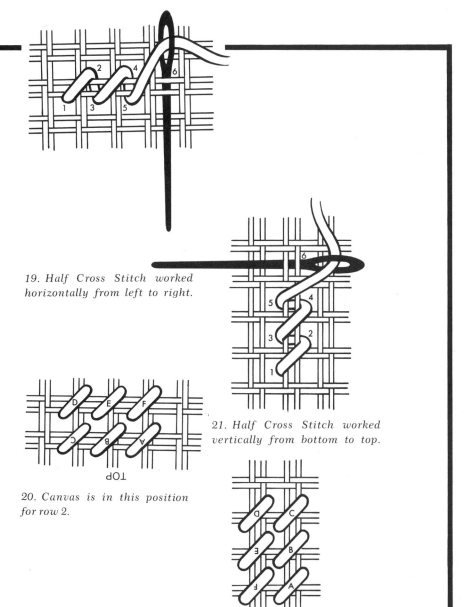

19. *Half Cross Stitch worked horizontally from left to right.*

20. *Canvas is in this position for row 2.*

21. *Half Cross Stitch worked vertically from bottom to top.*

22. *Canvas is in this position for row 2.*

Reversed Half Cross Stitch

Also called Half Cross Knitting Stitch

The Reversed Half Cross Stitch is made of two rows of Half Cross Stitch slanting in opposite directions (22). In appearance its ribbed effect resembles knitting. The ribs may be worked horizontally or vertically. Because the rows of stitches slant in opposite directions, some canvas may grin through. If your yarn is lightweight the situation will be aggravated, so try to select a proper weight yarn to cover the canvas. The Reversed Half Cross is a handy grounding stitch. It is worked on penelope only.

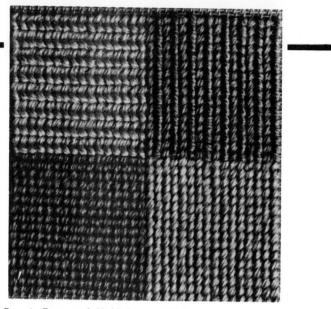

Box 1. *Reversed Half Cross Stitch worked in horizontal rows.*
Box 2. *Reversed Half Cross Stitch worked in vertical rows.*
Box 3. *Half Cross Stitch worked horizontally.*
Box 4. *Half Cross Stitch worked vertically.*
Note boxes 2 and 4, worked vertically, are more impressive and have better stitch definition. This sample is worked with 2-ply Persian on 11/22-mesh penelope.

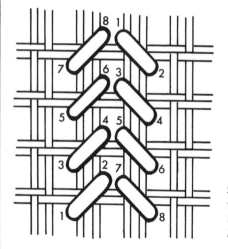

23. *Reversed Half Cross Stitch worked vertically, one row at a time, from top to bottom and bottom to top.*

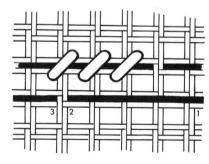

24. *Tramé under Half Cross Stitch on penelope.*

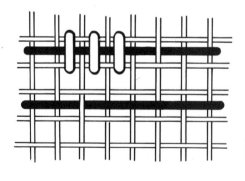

25. *Tramé under Straight Gobelin Stitch on mono.*

Tramé

Tramé is really a running stitch, but because it is usually associated with the Half Cross Stitch it is placed here with the slanting stitches. Very often a painted canvas from England will come with long horizontal threads of color worked over the design. These laid threads are called tramé and they tell the needle worker what color yarn to use. Customarily, Half Cross Stitch is worked over it in horizontal rows.

Tramé has the effect of fattening or "beefing up" stitches. It can be used under stitches that would look well padded. Make long running stitches at irregular intervals between the 2 threads of a horizontal row of penelope canvas or between 2 horizontal threads of mono. Use the same yarn as you plan to use to cover the area but 1 ply less. Stitches should be uneven in length and should be taken over no more than 7 stitches. There should be as little yarn on the back of the canvas as possible, so go under only 1 canvas thread between stitches.

The Tramé under the Straight Gobelin Stitch is worked in 2-ply Persian, the Gobelin itself in 3 ply. The Half Cross Tramé is 1 ply under 2. The canvas is 10/20-mesh penelope. Tramé is most often used on penelope.

Reversed Tent Stitch

Also called Knitting Tent Stitch

The Reversed Tent Stitch is like the Reversed Half Cross Stitch. It is made of two rows of stitches slanting in opposite directions. It may be worked horizontally (26) or vertically (27). Discretion should be exercised in the use of this stitch as it often results in an amateurish effect. Beginners always want to reverse the Tent Stitch when there is a line in their design that veers left because the Tent Stitch only makes lines that slant to the right; but unless this is done with skill, a hodge podge of directions results. This is not to say that there will not be times when you will want to reverse the direction of the Tent Stitch to emphasize a direction. To get an idea of some of the effects you can achieve, look at Letters I and X in the Alphabet Sampler.

Reversed Tent is a useful grounding stitch when worked in one color. A herringbone stripe in two colors can be used to create a pattern. Select a proper weight yarn to cover the canvas sufficiently; because the two rows of stitches slant in opposite directions, the canvas between the rows may be exposed.

Alternate boxes of horizontal and vertical Reversed Tent Stitch are worked in 3-ply Persian on 10-mesh mono.

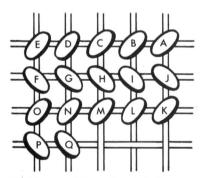

26. *Reversed Tent Stitch in horizontal rows.*

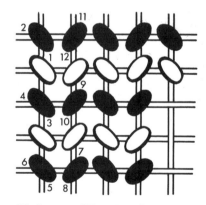

27. *Reversed Tent Stitch in vertical rows, alternating colors. The horizontal herringbone stripe is made by skipping every other stitch and then filling them in with another color.*

Rep Stitch

Also called Aubusson Stitch

This is an unusual grounding stitch that looks like a Rep fabric or an Aubusson tapestry. It is a very appropriate stitch for period or modern hangings. It is worked on penelope canvas and uses both of the double horizontal canvas threads individually, but it does not split the 2 vertical threads. A fine, textured stitch is achieved without the tedium of pricking apart the double vertical canvas threads as you would for petit point. Work it in vertical rows as shown in diagram 28. Turn work with each row. Rep Stitch may also be worked in diagonal rows; it makes a basket weave on the back of the canvas.

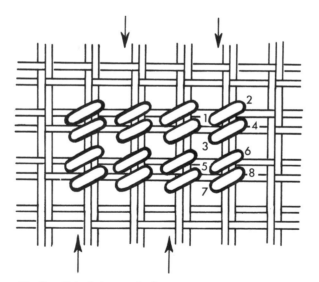

28. Rep Stitch in vertical rows.

The Rep Stitch is worked in boxes in 2-ply Persian on 10/20-mesh penelope.

Slanting Gobelin Stitch

*Also called Sloping Gobelin Stitch
and Oblique Gobelin Stitch*

The Slanting Gobelin Stitch is actually a big Tent Stitch worked over 2, 3, 4, or 5 horizontal canvas threads and over 1, 2, or 3 vertical canvas threads, in any combination of these. Work one row from right to left and the next from left to right, following the numbers in the diagrams. If it is easier, however, the work may be turned with each row and all rows worked in the same direction. Remember while doing the Slanting Gobelin to be consistent in your stitch count. The stitch count is the determined number of horizontal and vertical threads over which the stitch is taken. Beginners commonly lose their original count in this stitch and the result is very uneven. Consistently go over the same number of horizontal and vertical canvas threads within each row.

Notice in the diagrams 29, 30, and 33 that Tent Stitches are taken at the beginning and end of each row. They are compensating stitches used to cover the bare canvas thread that would otherwise be exposed.

The Slanting Gobelin works equally well in a vertical direction. It is useful for geometric designs, for borders, and for quickly worked backgrounds. For a lush grassy background for animals on pictures or pillows, try 2 values of green wool and slant the stitch over 1 vertical canvas thread as in diagrams 31 and 32.

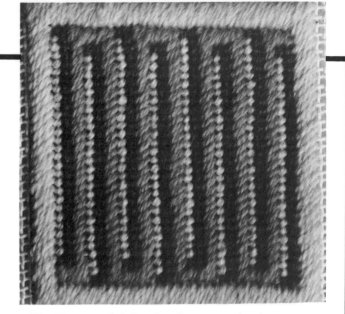

The Slanting Gobelin Stitch creates the design on this 12-mesh mono canvas. The Gobelin is worked in 3-ply Persian for a raised effect; the Tent Stitch ground is worked in 2 ply. Notice how the upper left and lower right corners are treated. Large diagonal compensating stitches are used to avoid a break where the 2 sides meet.

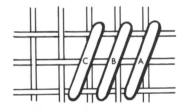

32. *Slanting Gobelin over 3 horizontal by 1 vertical canvas thread.*

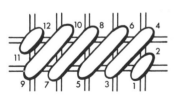

29. *Slanting Gobelin Stitch over 2 horizontal by 2 vertical canvas threads.*

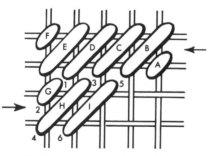

30. *Row 1 worked from right to left; row 2 worked from left to right.*

31. *Slanting Gobelin Stitch over 2 horizontal by 1 vertical canvas thread.*

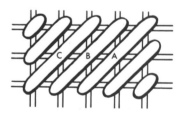

33. *Slanting Gobelin over 3 horizontal by 3 vertical canvas threads. Note the compensating stitches at either end of the row.*

Kalem Stitch

Also called Knitting Gobelin Stitch

Kalem Stitch resembles knitting even more than Reversed Tent Stitch, and it is easier than the Chain Stitch, another stitch that resembles knitting.

For a vertical knit effect work from the top of the canvas down for one row and from the bottom up for the next row; it is not necessary to turn the canvas. Stitches are taken over 1 vertical by 2 horizontal canvas threads (34).

For a horizontal knit effect work from side to side following the numbers in the diagram. Stitches are now taken over 2 vertical by 1 horizontal canvas thread (35).

The Kalem Stitch worked in blended colors makes a flat but patterned grounding (see Letter G in the Alphabet Sampler).

Rows of horizontal and vertical Kalem Stitch criss-cross Tent; worked in 2-ply Persian on 12-mesh mono.

34. *Kalem Stitch in vertical rows.*

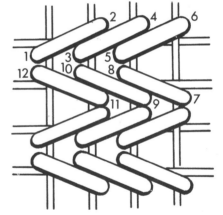

35. *Kalem Stitch in horizontal rows.*

57

Encroaching Gobelin Stitch

The Encroaching Gobelin is a variation of the Slanting Gobelin Stitch. The second row of stitches overlaps or encroaches into the row above. The encroaching must be done in a very cautious manner, consistently poking the needle through the canvas to the right of the stitch in the row above without splitting the stitch with the needle. In diagram 36 the rows are worked in alternate directions, but they can also be worked by turning the canvas after each row and working all rows from right to left.

Use the Encroaching Gobelin Stitch in small areas rather than attempting a whole background since it tends to distort the canvas. The overlapping makes it excellent for subtle shading, particularly for fur and feathers. The Encroaching Gobelin is used for the bird in the Genesis Sampler on pages 2–3 of photo insert.

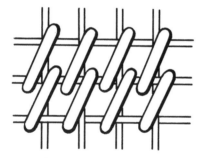

37. *Encroaching Gobelin Stitch over 1 vertical by 3 horizontal canvas threads.*

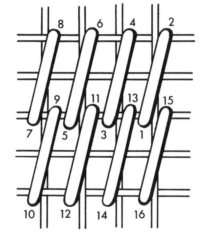

36. *Encroaching Gobelin Stitch over 1 vertical by 2 horizontal canvas threads.*

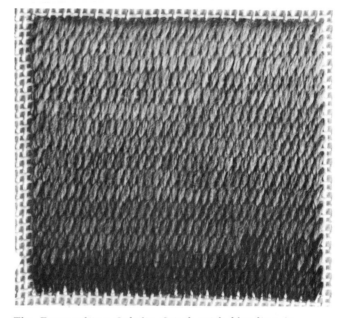

The Encroaching Gobelin Stitch with blending is worked in 2-ply Persian on 12-mesh mono.

Stem Stitch

Stem Stitch is a combination of Slanting Gobelin Stitch and Back Stitch. The diagram shows the Gobelin Stitch taken over 2 vertical by 2 horizontal canvas threads. The Back Stitch is taken over 2 horizontal canvas threads although it may also be taken over 1.

Note that two numbering systems are shown. The one on the left takes a bigger stitch on the back to create a heavier fabric; the one on the right takes a shorter stitch on the back for a thinner fabric.

The Gobelin Stitch is put in first and then the Back Stitch. The Back Stitch may be emphasized by using contrasting color or texture (see Letter T in the Alphabet Sampler).

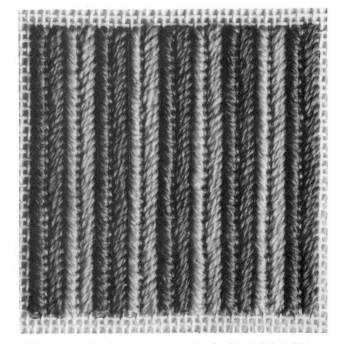

The Stem Stitch is worked in 2-ply Persian on 12-mesh mono; Back Stitches are taken over 1 horizontal canvas thread.

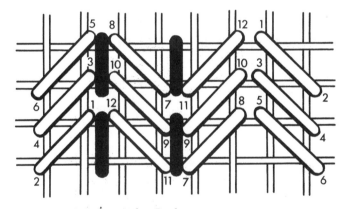

38. Stem Stitch with Back Stitch taken over 2 canvas threads.

Leaf Stitch

Leaf Stitch may seem complicated at first attempt but after making a few leaf units it becomes quite simple.

1. Start at the top of the leaf with a straight stitch over 3 horizontal canvas threads—out 1, in 2.
2. Skip 1 canvas thread below this stitch and come out at 3. Three stitches are then taken one below the other, fanning out to points 4, 6, and 8.
3. The next 2 stitches are the same as the last and are taken directly beneath each other over the same thread count.

4. Repeat the same formula on the other side of the leaf; start out 13, in 14.
5. Start the next leaf in line with the top of the first, leaving 6 vertical canvas threads between the two tops.
6. After the leaves are done make the stems with a straight stitch worked in a darker value or a different color. The next row of leaves is positioned with the first stitch between two leaves in the row above.

Several Leaf Stitches can be grouped in an arrangement (see Letter T in the Alphabet Sampler); rows in varying colors or values (see Letter B) can make an all-over pattern; or a single row can be used as a border.

Horizontal rows of Leaf Stitch are worked in 3-ply Persian on 12-mesh mono.

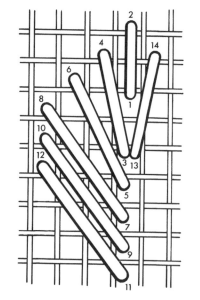

39. Half of the Leaf Stitch unit is worked from the top of the leaf down, then the second half is worked as the first.

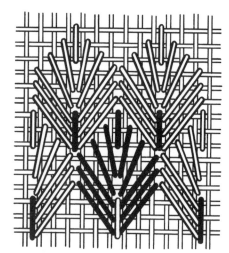

40. Interlocking horizontal rows of Leaf Stitch.

Mosaic Stitch

Also called Diagonal Hungarian Stitch

The Mosaic Stitch is a unit of 3 stitches: a Tent Stitch, a Slanting Gobelin Stitch, and another Tent Stitch (41).

It may be worked in horizontal rows from right to left (42), in vertical rows from the top down (turning the work with each row) (43), and in diagonal rows (44).

The Mosaic Stitch worked diagonally causes less distortion than the horizontal or vertical method. Once you have mastered the diagonal Tent Stitch you will find it easy to do. Work in diagonal rows. Complete each unit before starting the next unit.

The Mosaic Stitch is an excellent choice of grounding stitch to use with Tent because the compensating stitches are Tent Stitches and they will blend with the design. Experiment with alternate rows of different colors or values for a checkered effect.

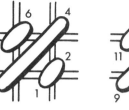
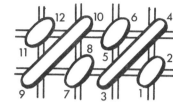
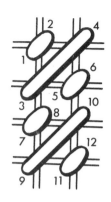

41. Mosaic Stitch worked from the lower right corner.

42. Mosaic Stitch worked horizontally.

43. Mosaic Stitch worked vertically.

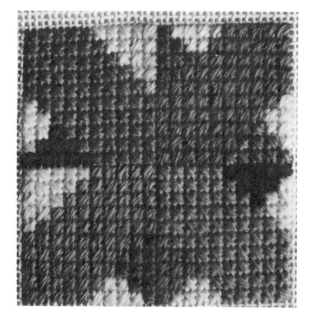

The Mosaic Stitch, slanting in 2 directions, is worked in 2-ply Persian on 14-mesh mono.

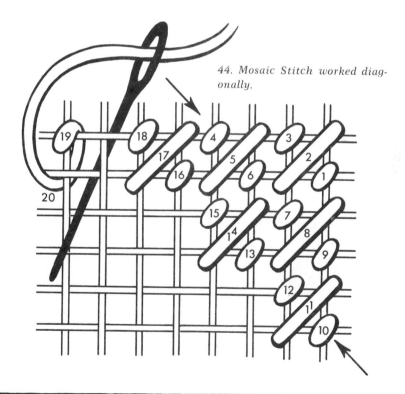

44. Mosaic Stitch worked diagonally.

Continuous Mosaic Stitch

Also called Florence Stitch
and Diagonal Florentine Stitch

The Continuous Mosaic Stitch is worked in diagonal rows. It is a handsome grounding stitch although it does distort the canvas somewhat even though it is worked diagonally. Blocking will straighten the canvas, however. The stitch is quite simple: a short and a long stitch alternate in both diagonal directions. However, maintaining straight edges is difficult until a recipe is created for the placement of compensating stitches. A recipe for a stitch count of 1 and 2 (Tent Stitch taken over 1 vertical and horizontal thread, Slanting Gobelin over 2) is shown in diagram 48.

A woven straw look (with a diagonal appearance) can easily be simulated by making the smaller stitch in a darker value (see the basket in the Genesis Sampler on pages 2–3 of photo insert).

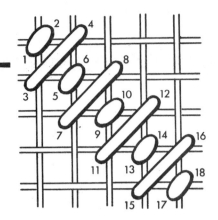

45. *Continuous Mosaic Stitch with stitch count of 1 and 2.*

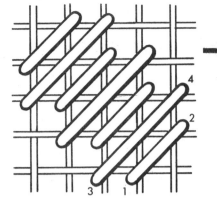

46. *Continuous Mosaic Stitch with stitch count of 2 and 3.*

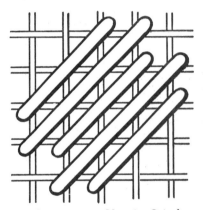

47. *Continuous Mosaic Stitch with stitch count of 3 and 4.*

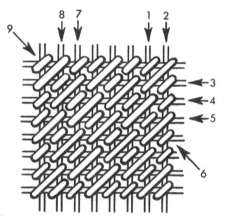

48. *Recipe for adding compensating stitches to make straight edges. Follow from the top of the first Mosaic Stitch.*
1. *Tent Stitch.*
2. *Gobelin Stitch.*
3. *Tent Stitch.*
4. *Compensating Tent Stitch.*
5. *Skip this canvas thread.*
6. *Tent Stitch, Gobelin Stitch, Tent Stitch: alternate the two until end of diagonal row.*
7. *Compensating Tent Stitch.*
8. *Skip this canvas thread.*
9. *Tent Stitch, Gobelin Stitch, Tent Stitch: alternate the two until end of second diagonal row.*

The Continuous Mosaic Stitch, slanting in 2 directions, is shown on a Tent Stitch ground with a Diamond Eyelet in the center. The wool is 2-ply Persian and the canvas is 12-mesh mono.

Small Chequer Stitch

The Small Chequer Stitch is a combination of units of Mosaic Stitch and boxes of Tent Stitch. The Mosaic Stitch is worked in diagonal rows, skipping a set of canvas threads between each row which is later filled in with Tent Stitch. It is a good grounding stitch and is striking in two colors or values (see Letter H of the Alphabet Sampler).

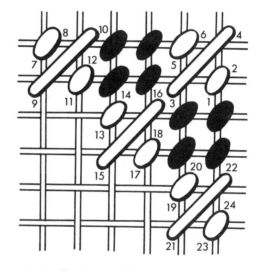

49. Small Chequer Stitch.

The Small Chequer Stitch is worked in 3-ply Persian on 10-mesh mono.

Cashmere Stitch

The Cashmere Stitch is an enlarged Mosaic Stitch made with the addition of a second Slanting Gobelin (50). Units are made of 4 instead of 3 stitches. Cashmere Stitch may be worked in horizontal or vertical rows, or in diagonal rows for less distortion. It is a good grounding stitch that looks like fabric. Boxes (units) can be worked in different colors or values as in Letter X of the Alphabet Sampler.

Continuous Cashmere Stitch

The Continuous Cashmere Stitch eliminates one of the smaller stitches of the Cashmere Stitch unit as it travels up and down the canvas in diagonal rows. Each diagonal row drops one canvas thread as it repeats the last diagonal row. Compensating stitches can be put in afterwards to make straight edges.

Two rows of horizontal and vertical Cashmere Stitch outline an area of Continuous Cashmere Stitch in 2-ply Persian on 12-mesh mono.

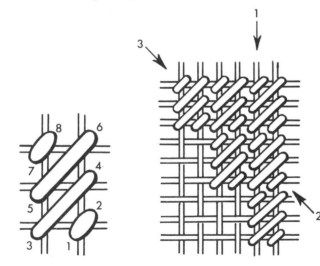

50. Units of Cashmere Stitch worked horizontally are begun at base of the unit; units worked vertically are begun at the top. Turn work with each row or reverse order in which stitches are taken.

51. Start a vertical row or a corner of a diagonal row at 1.
   First stitch of first (ascending) diagonal row starts at 2.
   First stitch of second (descending) diagonal row starts at 3.

52. Diagonal rows are worked alternately from top to bottom and bottom to top. Note on every other row units of Cashmere Stitch are parallel.

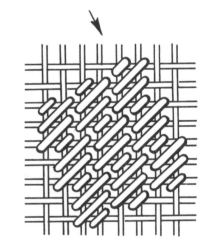

Flat Stitch

Also called Diagonal Satin Stitch and Scotch Stitch

The Flat Stitch is a square unit of 5 or 7 slanting stitches worked over 3 by 3 (53) or 4 by 4 canvas threads (54). It may be worked in horizontal or vertical rows; however, it does distort the canvas, so when covering large areas, work in diagonal rows.

For a checkered effect with alternate boxes slanting in opposite directions, work in one direction, skipping every other set of diagonal rows (55). When you are ready to work in the other direction, give the canvas half a turn so the top is at the side (56). Your stitches will now travel in the opposite direction. Alternate diagonal rows can be worked in two colors or two values of the same color. An Upright Cross Stitch in a third color can be used to fill the exposed mesh between the corners of the boxes. This is an easy and practical stitch. It makes a quilted fabric, striking for borders and backgrounds. It is used for the Ribbon Pillow on page 35.

This is a detail from the Ribbon Pillow on page 35. On either side of the Flat Stitches are 2 rows of Tent Stitch and 1 of Slanting Gobelin. The background is Tent. Three-ply Persian is used on 10-mesh mono. The horizontal band of ribbon is worked first. The canvas is then given a quarter turn so that the top becomes the side, and the vertical band is worked. This creates the wavy effect and makes the vertical and horizontal bands slant in different directions.

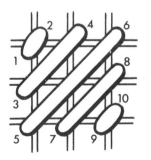

53. *Flat Stitch over 3 horizontal by 3 vertical canvas threads.*

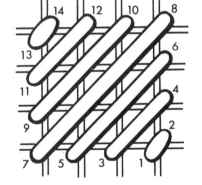

54. *Flat Stitch over 4 horizontal by 4 vertical canvas threads with 7 stitches to the unit.*

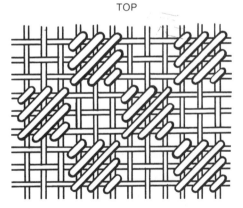

55. *To work alternate rows in opposite directions, first complete work in one direction.*

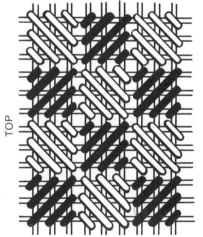

56. *Then turn canvas so top is on the side; fill in remaining rows.*

Cushion Stitch

The Cushion Stitch is an embellished Flat Stitch. It is a very useful stitch and easy to master. Two Flat Stitches are made in a diagonal row, then a long stitch is laid between them (57). The canvas is then given a quarter turn so the top becomes the side and a second set of Flat Stitches is made over the laid stitch (58). The Cushion Stitch makes a nice solid background or wide border.

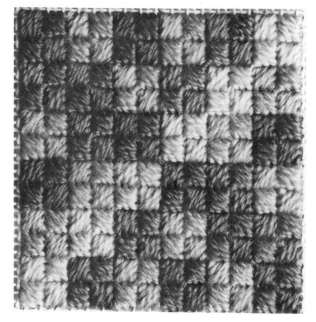

Boxes of Cushion Stitch are worked in 2-ply Persian on 12-mesh mono.

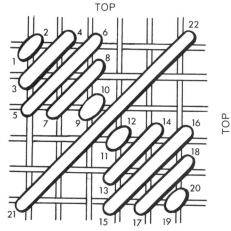

57. Two Flat Stitches are made, then a long stitch.

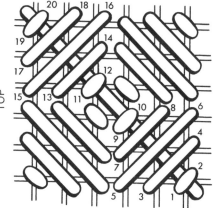

58. With the top at the side, 2 Flat Stitches are made over the long stitch.

Large Chequer Stitch

The Large Chequer Stitch alternates Flat Stitch with boxes of Tent Stitch. The Flat Stitch is worked diagonally, skipping a set of canvas threads which is filled in later with Tent Stitches. It is very easy to do and especially attractive in two colors.

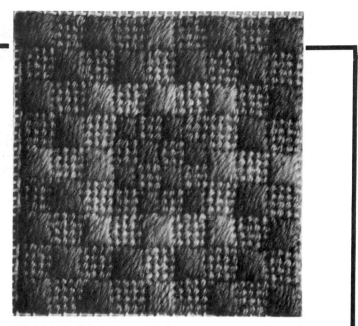

The Large Chequer Stitch is worked in 2 sizes on 12-mesh mono. Stitches in the interior section are worked over an area of 3 horizontal by 3 vertical canvas threads; the rest is worked over 4 by 4. The Flat Stitch portion uses 3-ply Persian and the Tent Stitch is worked in 2 ply.

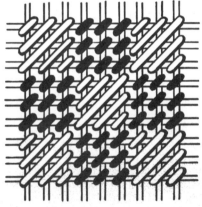

59. Large Chequer Stitch over 3 horizontal by 3 vertical canvas threads.

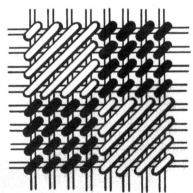

60. Large Chequer Stitch over 4 horizontal by 4 vertical canvas threads.

Scottish Stitch

The Scottish Stitch is a Flat Stitch outlined with Tent Stitch. To avoid distortion lay the Tent Stitch first, in step formation (61), and then fill in the squares with Flat Stitch worked in diagonal rows (62).

If you are working the outline and Flat Stitch in the same color, lay the Flat Stitch first, putting in the corner stitch before and after each unit as shown in diagram 63.

The Flat Stitch can be taken over 3 or 4 canvas threads. For an interesting effect, reverse the direction of the stitch in every other row.

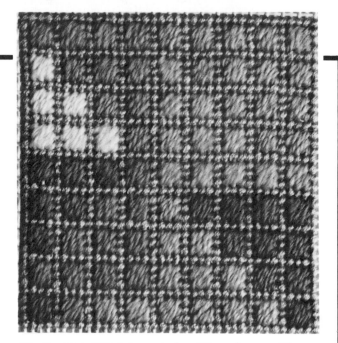

The Scottish Stitch is worked on 12-mesh mono. The Flat Stitch portion uses 2-ply Persian; the Tent outline, 7-ply French silk.

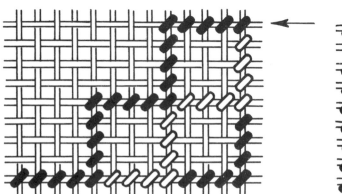

61. Notice the Tent Stitch outline is worked in steps.

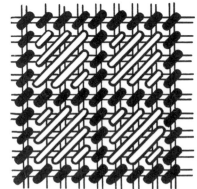

62. Flat Stitch fills in the outlined spaces.

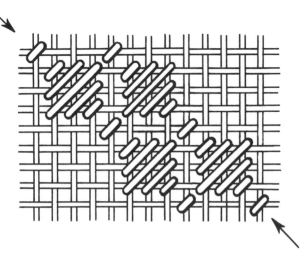

63. With one color, the Flat Stitch is worked first and the corner Tent Stitches are filled in simultaneously.

Continuous Flat Stitch

Also called Diagonal Stitch

The Continuous Flat Stitch travels up and down the canvas in diagonal rows over 2, 3, 4, 3 canvas threads for each repeat. Note, in the diagram, the longest stitches in one row are diagonally opposite the shortest stitches in the next diagonal row.

The Continuous Flat Stitch makes a rich brocade fabric. It is especially handsome worked in bold stripes of color.

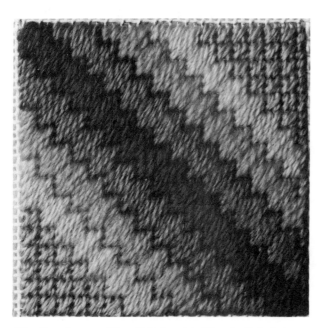

The Continuous Flat Stitch with Mosaic Stitch in 2 corners is worked in 2-ply Persian on 12-mesh mono.

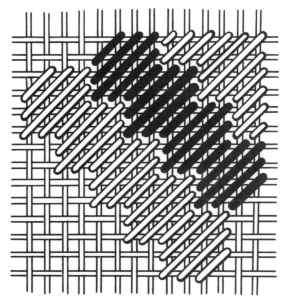

64. *Note that compensating stitches are worked at top and side of the first row to make straight edges.*

Moorish Stitch

The Moorish Stitch is a variation of the Continuous Flat Stitch. A row of Continuous Flat Stitch (2,3,4,3) is made and outlined on either side with steps of Tent Stitch. This is an attractive grounding stitch that may be worked in contrasting textures and colors. It is used in Letters E and Y of the Alphabet Sampler.

The Moorish Stitch is worked in 2-ply Persian and 1 strand of pearl cotton on 12-mesh mono.

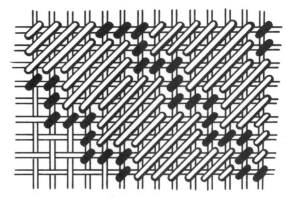

65. Compensating stitches have been taken to keep edges straight. Notice Tent Stitch steps are made of 3 stitches in each direction.

Byzantine Stitch

The Byzantine Stitch is the easiest of the following group of zigzag stitches. It may be started in the corner over a box of 3 or 4 canvas threads as shown in diagram 66. Diagonal rows of stitches are then worked in steps across the canvas. Count over 8 canvas threads to the left of the corner stitch and start a Flat Stitch. When you reach the corner of the first Flat Stitch, start to work a vertical row. A consistent pattern of 5 horizontally placed and 5 vertically placed stitches will emerge to guide you. (I worked it over 3 canvas threads with a count of 4 stitches to each step on My Vest which appears on page 38.) You may start anywhere on the canvas by establishing one row and following its course.

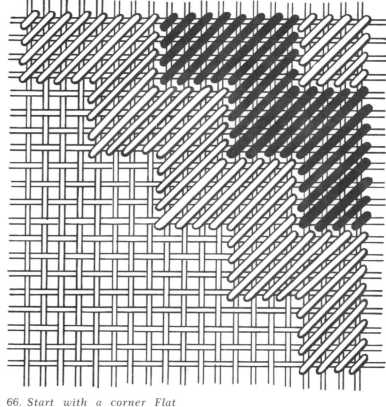

The Byzantine Stitch is worked over 4 canvas threads in 2-ply Persian on 12-mesh mono.

66. *Start with a corner Flat Stitch over 4 horizontal by 4 vertical canvas threads.*

Jacquard Stitch

The Jacquard Stitch is composed of steps of Slanting Gobelin Stitch outlined with Tent Stitch. The Slanting Gobelin is worked over 2 by 2 canvas threads in steps of a constant, predetermined number of stitches. Diagram 65 has a count of 5 stitches to a step, while My Vest on page 38 uses 4 stitches to a step. Steps of 6 and 7 stitches are also possible. Compensating Tent Stitches are used to make straight edges and fill in any blank canvas threads.

On mono canvas, you will have to do some maneuvering to work the Tent Stitch steps from left to right. On the horizontal planes, come out at the top of the stitch instead of the base. On the vertical planes, Tent Stitch as usual. On penelope there is no problem. Work horizontal planes in Half Cross Stitch and vertical planes in Tent Stitch.

The Jacquard Stitch is worked 5 stitches to a step in 2-ply Persian and 7-ply French silk on 12-mesh mono.

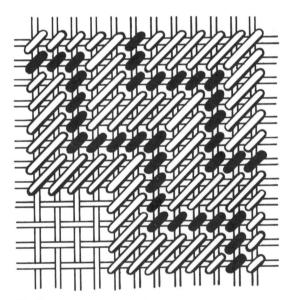

67. Compensating stitches are taken to keep straight edges.

Milanese Stitch

The Milanese Stitch may be thought of as half of a Flat Stitch. Each unit is made of four stitches. The units look like arrowheads and are worked diagonally across the canvas, each row pointing in the opposite direction. Notice in diagram 68 that the shortest stitch in one row is always diagonally opposite the longest stitch in the next row. Compensating stitches fill in open mesh in the upper right corner. The Milanese Stitch can be worked in one or two colors. It is used in Letter Z of the Alphabet Sampler.

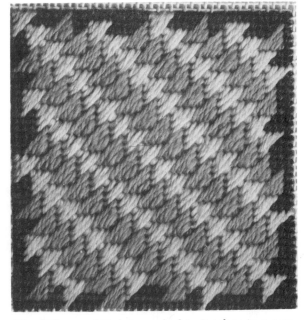

The Milanese Stitch is worked in 2 colors in a novelty cotton thread on 14-mesh mono. No compensating stitches are taken in this case; instead, all open areas are filled with Tent Stitch in a contrasting color of 2-ply Persian.

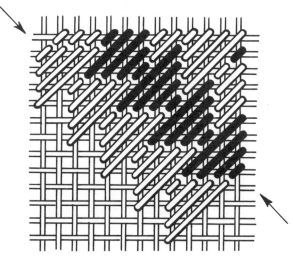

68. Tent Stitch is the first stitch of the unit of 4 stitches.

Oriental Stitch

The Oriental Stitch is a Milanese Stitch with Slanting Gobelin between each diagonal row. Notice that the longest stitch in one row is diagonally opposite the longest stitch in the next row. Arrowheads point in opposite directions. Set in the Milanese rows first, then fill in the remaining canvas threads with Slanting Gobelin in a contrasting color. The Oriental Stitch may be seen in Letter W of the Alphabet Sampler.

The Oriental Stitch is worked in 2-ply Persian on 12-mesh mono. Instead of compensating stitches, the open areas are filled with additional Gobelin Stitches.

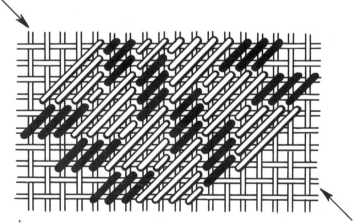

69. Slanting Gobelin Stitches are worked horizontally in one diagonal row and vertically in the next.

74

Algerian Eye Stitch

Also called Star Stitch

The Algerian Eye Stitch is a unit of 8 stitches. Each stitch of the unit is taken over 2 canvas threads (70). Start with a straight stitch and work clockwise. The needle always goes in at the center to accentuate the eyelet hole (71). When working a series of Algerian Eye, be consistent in the formation of the stitch so that all units look exactly alike. This stitch is most easily worked on penelope canvas. It is most effective as a mini stitch, using each of the double canvas threads individually. On 12-mesh mono try using 2-ply Persian, working each stitch twice before moving on to the next stitch of the unit. Pull each stitch tightly for a pronounced eyelet in the center. Complete each unit by pulling the yarn snugly through the backs of the stitches, taking care not to cover the eyelet, and proceed to the next unit. Alternate units of Algerian Eye and Flat Stitch makes an unusual all-over design (72).

Alternate units of Algerian Eye and Flat Stitch border Tent Stitch. The Algerian Eye is worked in 3-ply Persian, the other stitches in French linen, on 14-mesh mono.

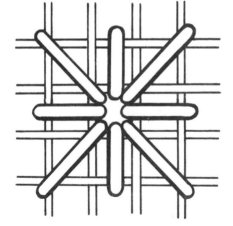

70. *Algerian Eye Stitch over 4 horizontal by 4 vertical canvas threads.*

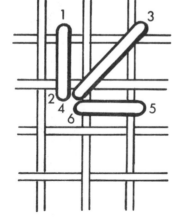

71. *Work all stitches clockwise going into the center hole.*

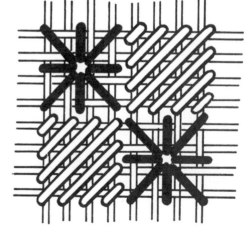

72. *Alternate units of Algerian Eye and Flat Stitch.*

Eyelet Stitch

The Eyelet Stitch uses every mesh opening around the perimeter of the square that defines it. Work each unit in the same direction starting with a vertical or horizontal stitch. All stitches are taken over the same number of canvas threads and go into the same center hole to form the eyelet. End each unit by snugly pulling the thread through the stitches on the back of the canvas, taking care not to block the eyelet. This is a very important looking stitch, excellent for dramatic accent.

Diamond Eyelet Stitch

Also called Diagonal Star Stitch

The Diamond Eyelet Stitch is another dramatic stitch and combines nicely with other stitches. All units should be worked in the same direction, starting with a vertical stitch at the bottom. All stitches go into the same center hole to form the eyelet. End off each unit by snugly pulling the thread through the stitches on the back, taking care not to block the eyelet. The Diamond Eyelet is used in Letter B of the Alphabet Sampler and on the Eyelet Stitch swatch.

The Eyelet and Diamond Eyelet are worked on a Tent background. The Eyelet and the entire swatch are outlined with Slanting Gobelin Stitch. Notice that rayon is used to accent the center and to Back Stitch around the Eyelet. The rest is worked in 2-ply Persian. The canvas is 12-mesh mono.

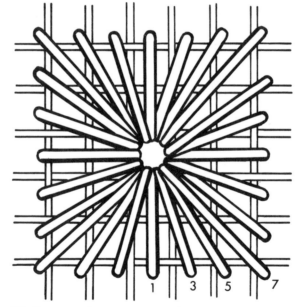

73. *Every mesh opening is used to make a square. All stitches of the unit are taken into the central mesh opening.*

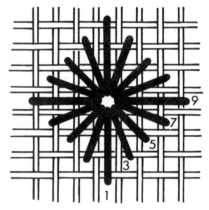

74. *Every mesh opening is used to make a diamond. All stitches of the unit are taken into the central mesh opening.*

Straight Stitches

Straight Gobelin Stitch
Brick Stitch
Back Stitch
Parisian Stitch
Hungarian Stitch
Hungarian Diamond
Triangle Stitch
Florentine Embroidery
  Florentine Stitch
  Bargello

Straight Gobelin Stitch

Also called Upright Gobelin and Gobelin Droit

The Straight Gobelin Stitch is easy to learn. It is a vertical stitch worked over horizontal rows of 2, 3, 4 or more canvas threads. Work alternate rows in opposite directions, from left to right, then right to left. Start each stitch by coming up through the canvas at the base of the stitch and go in at the top (75).

Most straight stitches worked in rows leave exposed canvas threads between the rows. Keep an even, loose tension and use a full strand of yarn to minimize the grin-through. A Back Stitch in a matching or contrasting color in a lighter weight yarn can be worked between the rows to cover any exposed canvas.

Because the Straight Gobelin can be worked in two directions— over vertical and horizontal canvas threads—it may be used to turn corners, making it a perfect stitch for borders. If a very padded look is desired, a tramé thread can be laid in irregular lengths beneath it. The Straight Gobelin looks particularly well in rows shaded from light to dark.

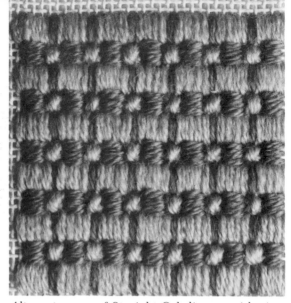

Alternate rows of Straight Gobelin, over 4 horizontal and 3 vertical canvas threads, are shown. The horizontal stitches have Smyrna Stitches between each unit. Three-ply Persian is used throughout on 12-mesh mono.

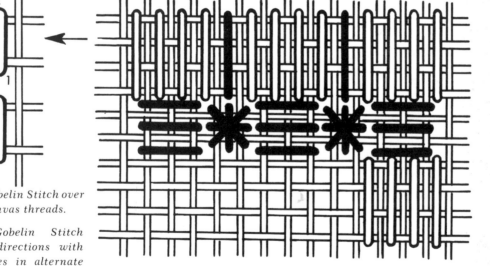

75. Straight Gobelin Stitch over 2 horizontal canvas threads.

76. Straight Gobelin Stitch worked in 2 directions with Smyrna Stitches in alternate rows.

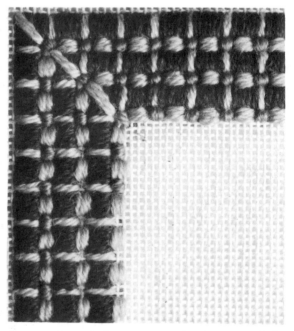

A corner is made by reversing the direction of the stitches.

Brick Stitch

The Brick Stitch is a series of Straight Gobelin Stitches taken over 2 or 4 canvas threads and laid in staggered rows like bricks. The stitch can be worked vertically (77) or horizontally (78). Vertical stitches are worked in horizontal rows from left to right and right to left. Horizontal stitches are worked in vertical rows from bottom up and top down. The first row skips a space between each stitch. This space is used by the second row of stitches which are taken between the stitches of the first row. In this way the rows interlock. Compensating stitches may be laid in afterwards or anticipated and made as larger stitches in advance. Brick Stitch makes an excellent background stitch and is a good choice for shading and blending.

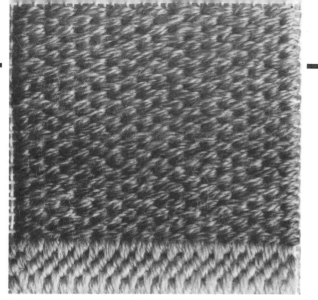

The horizontal Brick Stitch, taken over 4 vertical canvas threads, is blended for a skylike effect. At the base, shaded vertical Brick is worked over 2 horizontal canvas threads. Three-ply Persian is used on 12-mesh mono.

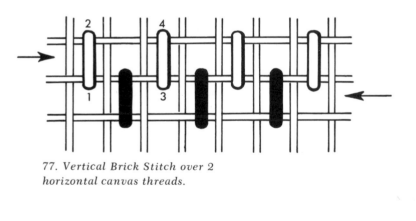

77. Vertical Brick Stitch over 2 horizontal canvas threads.

78. Horizontal Brick Stitch over 4 vertical canvas threads.

Back Stitch

Most people know the Back Stitch from sewing. It is especially useful for canvas work, particularly where subtle blending is required. The needle is drawn through the canvas at the far end of the stitch and back tracks to close it. It makes long stitches on the back of the work, longer than those on the front of the canvas. Remember, in looking over the diagrams, that odd numbers come out to the front of the canvas and even numbers go down through the canvas. This stitch is a big yarn eater and makes a thick mat when used for grounding.

The Back Stitch can be used over 1 or 2 canvas threads between rows of stitches for added decoration or to cover grin-through (80). It can be used to outline areas (for turning corners see 79). It can be used to cover a solid area for a tapestrylike quality (82). However, on mono canvas, Back Stitch covers the canvas best when staggered like Brick Stitch (81). On penelope canvas the stitches can be made in even rows like Gobelin. In this case, all horizontal spaces are used but the two closely woven vertical canvas threads are treated as one thread (82). Be careful not to draw the yarn too tightly when working large, solid areas of Back Stitch as the tension draws the canvas threads together and makes the canvas buckle.

The Back Stitch is worked in 2-ply Persian over 2 sets of vertical canvas threads using every space between the horizontal canvas threads. A heavy ribbed fabric results. The canvas is 11/22-mesh penelope; 10/20 will work equally well and is more easily available.

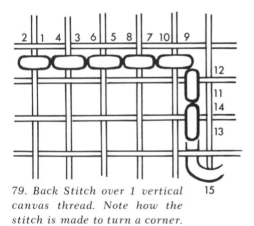

79. *Back Stitch over 1 vertical canvas thread. Note how the stitch is made to turn a corner.*

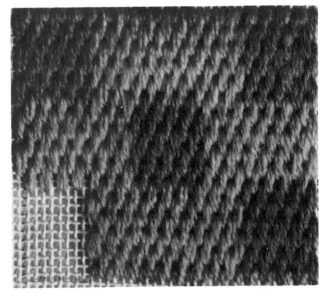

A staggered Back Stitch is taken over 4 horizontal canvas threads on 12-mesh mono. The checkered effect is created by using 2 values of the same color. The wool is 3-ply Persian.

This classic design uses bands of Back Stitch in 2 directions. The horizontal ribbons are stitched horizontally and the vertical ones vertically. The open spaces are filled with Straight Gobelin Stitch. Three-ply Persian is worked on the 14-mesh mono canvas.

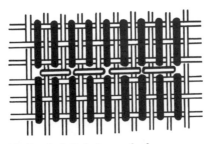

80. *Back Stitch is worked over 2 canvas threads to cover the grin-through between rows of Straight Gobelin Stitch. It can also be worked over 1 canvas thread.*

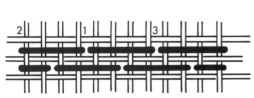

81. *Back Stitch used for a solid area. It is worked over 4 canvas threads and staggered, brick fashion, for better canvas coverage.*

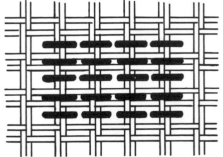

82. *Back Stitch on penelope canvas is worked over the closely woven vertical threads and between rows of open horizontal threads creating a ribbed effect. (See the man's overcoat in the Genesis Sampler on pages 2–3 of photo insert.)*

Parisian Stitch

The Parisian Stitch alternates long and short stitches along a row. The stitches can be worked vertically or horizontally over a series of 2 and 4 (83) or 3 and 1 canvas threads (85). The return row fits a short stitch under a long stitch and a long stitch under a short. Alternate the direction of rows, working from right to left, then left to right.

There are many ways to vary the Parisian Stitch and it is a very useful and popular stitch for this reason. The short stitches can be done in one color or type of yarn, the long stitches in another, in which case all the long stitches are put in first and the short ones later. Try different combinations of long and short; the accompanying diagrams illustrate some of the many variations.

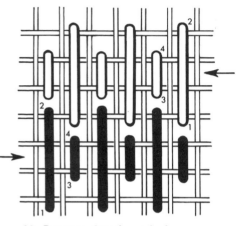

83. Parisian Stitch worked vertically over 4 and 2 horizontal canvas threads.

In the center a 2-color vertical Parisian Stitch variation is worked over 4 and 2 horizontal canvas threads. Surrounding it is an area of horizontal Parisian worked over 3 and 1 vertical canvas threads. The outermost band is Straight Gobelin with Flat Stitch corners. Three-ply Persian is used on 14-mesh mono.

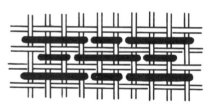

84. Parisian Stitch worked horizontally over 4 and 2 vertical canvas threads.

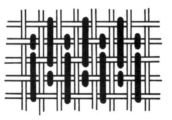

85. Parisian Stitch worked vertically over 3 and 1 horizontal canvas threads.

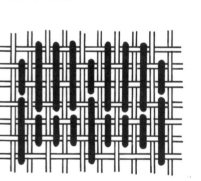

86. Parisian Stitch variation.

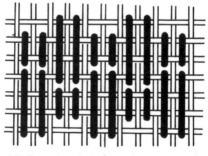

87. Parisian Stitch variation.

Hungarian Stitch

Also called Point d'Hungrie

The Hungarian Stitch is a unit of 3 stitches worked in a horizontal row. The first stitch of the unit is taken over 2 canvas threads and the second over 4; the third stitch completes the unit and is the same as the first. A space is skipped and then the next unit is begun (86).

Rows are worked in alternate directions, from left to right and right to left. Placement of the second row is a little confusing: the space to be skipped between units should be beneath the long stitches in the first row. Once you have completed the second row the rest is easy for every other row is identical. Take short stitches under short stitches and long stitches into the empty space between the units of the preceeding row.

There are many variations of the Hungarian Stitch. In diagram 89, two stitches of each length are made, creating a chainlike repeat.

Rows of Wave Stitch are filled in with Hungarian Stitch. This is sometimes called Hungarian Ground. Three-ply Persian is used on 12-mesh mono.

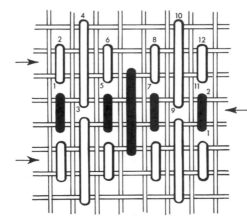

88. Hungarian Stitch worked in horizontal rows. The second row is shown in black for easy placement.

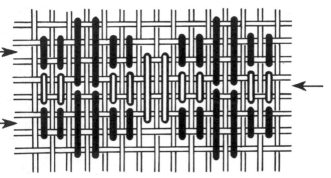

89. A Hungarian Stitch variation; each unit is composed of 6 stitches taken over 2,2,4,4,2,2 canvas threads.

In the center, 4 Hungarian Stitches slant in 2 directions and occupy the same center hole. Hungarian Diamonds surround the center unit on a field of Hungarian Stitch laid in horizontal rows. Compensating stitches are half Hungarian Diamonds. Three-ply Persian is used on 14-mesh mono.

83

Hungarian Diamond

The Hungarian Diamond is one of the many variations of the Hungarian Stitch. Each unit is composed of 5 or 7 stitches taken over 2, 4, 6, 4, 2 or 2, 4, 6, 8, 6, 4, 2 canvas threads.

Rows are worked in alternate directions from left to right and right to left. To work the stitch on its side, give the canvas a quarter turn. The Hungarian Diamond combines well with wave pattern.

The Hungarian Stitch and the Hungarian Diamond are used as filling stitches in a Wave Stitch design. Three-ply Persian is used on 12-mesh mono.

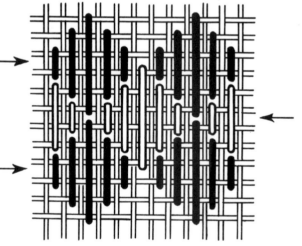

90. Hungarian Diamond; each unit is composed of 5 stitches taken over 2,4,6,4,2 canvas threads.

Above, *Ribbon pillow*: Worked by Mrs. Edward Ferree; instructions are on page 35. *Florentine Pillow*: Instructions are on page 36.

Right, *Basket of Flowers*: Instructions are on page 34.

Below, *Gingham Dog*: Instructions are on page 33.

Below right, *Chessboard*: Worked by Mrs. Alfred Yarkovsky; instructions are on page 33.

GENESIS SAMPLER

LADY ON THE RIGHT
  Blouse—St. George and St. Andrew Cross Stitch
  Blouse collar and trim—Rep Stitch and Cross Stitch
  Skirt—Long-armed Cross Stitch
  Apron—Tied Oblong Cross Stitch and Shell Stitch

GENTLEMAN
  Hat—Slanting Gobelin Stitch
  Vest—Jacquard Stitch
  Coat—Back Stitch, blended
  Trousers—Petit Point and Gros Point
  Boot—Tent Stitch

HORSE
  Body—Chain Stitch
  Saddle—Mosaic Stitch

LADY ON THE LEFT
  Bodice—Reversed Tent Stitch
  Collar—Continuous Mosaic Stitch and
    Slanting Gobelin Stitch
  Skirt—Cushion Stitch
  Apron—Kalem Stitch, Straight Gobelin Stitch,
    Mosaic Stitch, Double Cross Stitch, Turkey
    Knot Stitch

BIRD
  Encroaching Gobelin Stitch

BASKET
  Continuous Mosaic Stitch
  Straight Gobelin Stitch
  Wave Stitch

WATER
  Florentine Stitch

HOUSE
  Slanting Gobelin Stitch
  Brick Stitch

BUTTERFLY
  Smyrna Stitch
  Eyelet Stitch

TREE
  Trunk—French Stitch
  Foliage—Rococo Stitch

GRASS
  Florentine Stitch

BORDER
  Lettering—Slanting Gobelin Stitch
  Stripes—Slanting Gobelin Stitch
  Leaves—Leaf Stitch

*Most of the stitches used in the sampler are
done in miniature. The canvas is 11/22-mesh
penelope. The diagonal Tent Stitch background
is worked in 3-ply Persian; 3-ply French silk,
1-ply Persian, and 1-ply Nantucket Twist are
used for the petit point.*

Patchwork Pillow: Created by Patti Baker Russel; instructions are on page 37.

Far left, *My Vest: Instructions are on page 38.*
Left, *Persian Vest: Created by Patti Baker Russel; instructions are on page 34.*

Triangle Stitch

The Triangle Stitch is a fancy stitch that uses a box of 10 canvas threads. It is made of triangular units of Straight Gobelin Stitches. The first stitch is made over 2 horizontal canvas threads, the remaining over 3, 4, 5, 4, 3, 2. The canvas is then given a quarter turn and the second unit begun. After completing the four units, compensating stitches must be made in the corners. These corner stitches can be small Cross Stitches as shown in diagram 91, Smyrna Stitches, shown in Letter V of the Alphabet Sampler, or Mosaic Stitches, shown in the accompanying swatch. Back Stitch covers the exposed canvas threads between rows of Triangle Stitch.

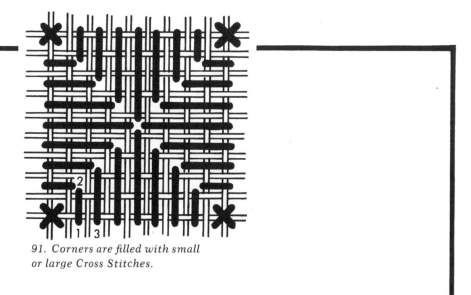

91. Corners are filled with small or large Cross Stitches.

This design uses a Triangle Stitch in the center which sets the direction for all of the stitches that follow—2 rows of Straight Gobelin outlined with Back Stitch and a border of interlocking triangles. Notice that all corners are mitered. Three-ply Persian is used for the Triangle Stitch, everything else is 2 ply. The canvas is 14-mesh mono.

After all Triangle Stitches are set in, 4 Mosaic Stitches are taken at each intersection, slanting toward the central mesh opening. Back Stitch over 5 canvas threads is put in last. Three-ply Persian is used on 14-mesh mono.

85

Florentine Embroidery

Florentine Embroidery is the name given to a whole specialized form of canvas work characterized by straight stitches of regulated length that rhythmically rise and fall to form zigzag designs.

Many Florentine patterns call for blocks of equal size stitches taken in a straight line. These designs should be stitched with a fuller thread and with looser tension. When the slightly loose stitches are pressed down in blocking or steaming they will cover any exposed canvas threads.

Mono canvas is most often used for Florentine Embroidery today. For best coverage on a 12- or 14-mesh canvas, 3-ply Persian should be used; on 10 mesh, 4 or 5 plies of Persian is needed. If you are unsure of the amount of yarn to use for a canvas, make a sample swatch to test various weights.

All Florentine Embroidery stitches come out to the front of the canvas at the base of the stitch and go in at the top. When descending a peak, a long stitch is made on the back of the canvas; when ascending, a short stitch is made; work rows in alternate directions so the back of the canvas gets an even distribution of wool. In this way your work will be flatter.

Since Florentine Embroidery is done by counting, a type of shorthand is sometimes used. The number of canvas threads that a stitch covers is given first, then the number of canvas threads, or steps, that it rises and falls. Example: 4.2 step means that stitches are taken over 4 canvas threads and each is begun 2 threads above or below the last.

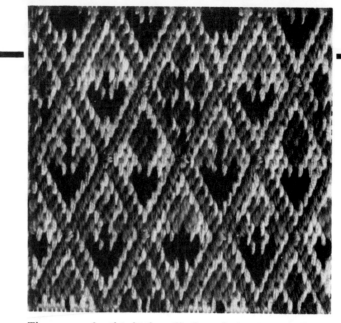

The canvas for this little mille fleur design is worked with the selvedges held at the top and bottom. All stitches are taken over 2 sets of closely woven canvas threads and rise and fall 1 set. At the intersection of the diamonds, Upright Cross Stitches are made with silk. The flowers and the diamond trellis are worked in 2-ply Persian, and the background in 7-ply French silk.

Florentine Stitch

Florentine Stitch is a style of Florentine Embroidery. Most often stitches are taken over 4 horizontal canvas threads that rise and fall 2 steps.

The carnation (see swatch) is a typical antique Florentine Stitch flower design in a 4.2 step. It is easier to copy directly from the swatch than from a diagram or graph. The background is worked in shaded rows of Florentine Stitch in the same 4.2 step but rising and falling in short peaks of 2 stitches.

The mille fleur design (see swatch and diagram 92) is a little repeat pattern of my own invention suitable for small or delicate items. Both the mille fleur and the carnation are worked on 10/20-mesh penelope canvas. The canvas is held so that the closely woven threads are in a horizontal position. By using all of the spaces between the now vertical canvas threads, and counting the closely woven double threads as 2 threads, a petit Florentine Stitch is made. Not only is a more delicate design possible with this method, but counting is greatly simplified.

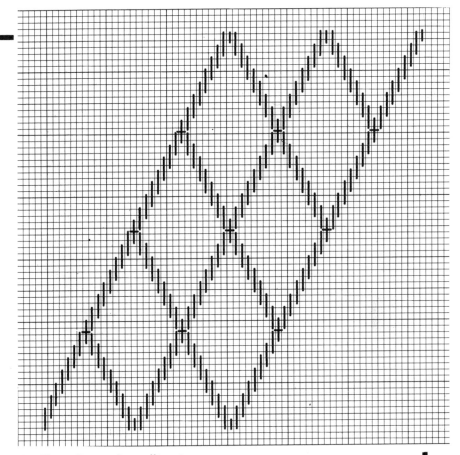

92. The diamond trellis is worked first, then the floral repeat and the background.

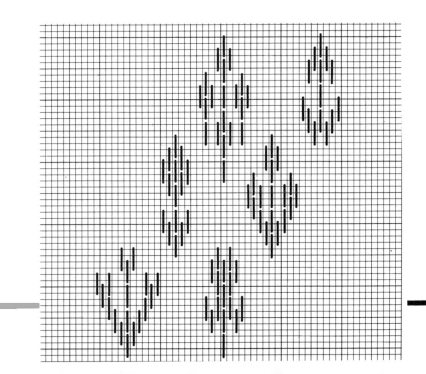

87

This carnation motif is a classic Florentine Stitch design. The outline is worked in 2-ply Persian and the filling in 7-ply French silk. The canvas, a 10/20-mesh penelope, is worked with the selvedges held at the top and bottom. All stitches are taken over 2 sets of closely woven canvas threads and rise and fall 1. The background is worked in 2-ply Persian. Although it resembles a Brick Stitch, it rises and falls like a Florentine Stitch.

Bargello

Bargello is another style of Florentine Embroidery. It is characterized by long stitches regularly interspersed with short stitches. The steps between the stitches are very short or very long. The short stitches are generally taken over 2 threads. A Bargello can be recognized by the secondary pattern that is made by the short stitches.

The wave pattern (93) is the simplest Bargello design. Each stitch rises 1 step; 4 ascending stitches are made, then 4 descending (count the first and last stitches each time). The next row is taken over 2 canvas threads and rises and falls 1 step.

To round the wave a block of stitches is made at the crest and at the base of the wave. The rounded waves in diagram 94 are made with a block of 3 stitches taken over 4 canvas threads. The second row is taken over 3 canvas threads.

The flame pattern (95) is another Bargello design. It consists of 1 long stitch and 4 short stitches in steps of 1. The long stitch is taken over 6 canvas threads, the short stitches over 2. The pattern is established in the first row and is repeated in the fifth with 4 intervening rows in between. Note that a vertical row of stitches (one stitch directly under the other) also establishes the repeat, in this case 1 long stitch and 4 short stitches.

To set up a Bargello, center the stitch in the first row of the repeat in the center of the canvas. Work the first row from the center to the left and then to the right in order to place the pattern evenly on the canvas. All other rows start at the right or left and alternate directions. If the design is being centered vertically, as well as horizontally, work rows from the center down. Reverse the canvas to complete.

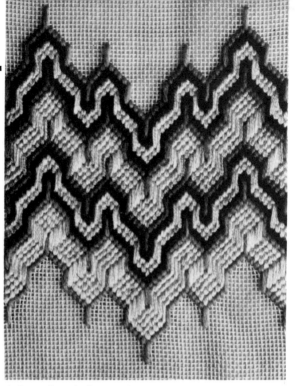

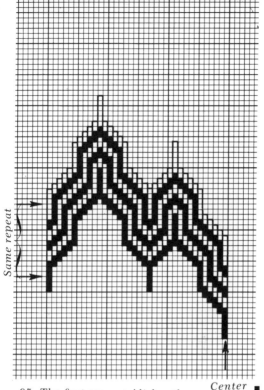

This is the same Bargello wave pattern shown in diagram 93 with the addition of a row of diamond openings which are made by reversing the direction of the wave. The diamond fillings are Hungarian Diamond and Diamond Eyelet. Three-ply Persian is used for all but the narrow waves, which are worked in heavy pearl cotton.

A formal and elegant flame effect is achieved with the use of a 24-mesh mono canvas. The 5-ply French silk and 2-ply Nantucket Twist are worked with a #22 needle.

95. The first row establishes the flame pattern. One long stitch is followed by 4 short stitches. Note that this same count emerges in the vertical rows of stitches as well.

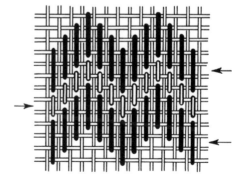

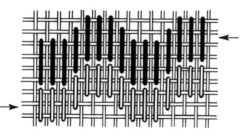

93. Note that the rows of waves are worked in alternate directions. When all rows are worked in the same direction, concentrations of thick and thin stitches form on the back of the canvas, creating pleats.

94. Blocks of stitches round the waves.

Cross Stitches

Cross Stitch
Upright Cross Stitch
St. George and St. Andrew Cross Stitch
Large and Upright Cross Stitch
Oblong Cross Stitch
Crossed Corners Stitch
Double Cross Stitch
Smyrna Stitch
Triple Cross Stitch
Leviathan Stitch
Long-armed Cross Stitch
Greek Stitch
Plait Stitch
Gobelin Plait Stitch

Cross Stitch

Also called Gros Point

The Cross Stitch is a unit of 2 stitches. The first slants from lower right to upper left (96). The second crosses the first and slants from lower left to upper right (97). The stitch is crossed in this order because the Cross Stitch and the Tent Stitch are often used together, and in such cases, they should both slant in the same direction. However, if no Tent is used, you can cross the stitch in either direction.

Cross Stitch is usually worked in horizontal rows. Each stitch can be crossed individually (98) or a whole row of the first half can be set in and then a return journey made to cross them (99, 100). This last method takes less time when covering a large area. They should be crossed individually when extra heavy coverage is required.

On penelope canvas, as shown in the diagrams, Cross Stitches cover each mesh. On mono canvas, however, 2 horizontal and 2 vertical canvas threads are used. The Cross Stitch is one of the easiest stitches; it is not necessary to turn the canvas or to work it diagonally, yet the work is never distorted. It makes a stout fabric and is an excellent choice for rugs. Since turning the canvas is not required, it is a good stitch for beginners.

96. *First half of the Cross Stitch.*

97. *Second half of the Cross Stitch.*

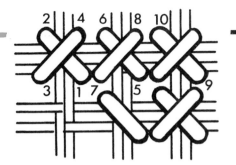

98. Stitches crossed individually.

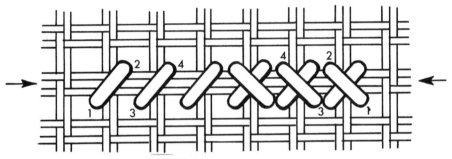

99. Working the first half of the stitch from left to right and returning to complete the row of stitches from right to left

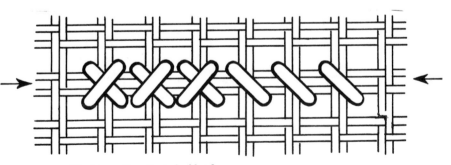

100. Working the first half of the stitch from right to left and returning to complete the row from left to right.

All stitches on this swatch are taken over 2 horizontal by 2 vertical canvas threads. Three-ply Persian is used on 12-mesh mono. Center square: Cross Stitch. Corner squares: St. George and St. Andrew Cross Stitch. Note that the top stitch of the St. Andrew slants toward the center. In the upper right corner, the St. George is crossed with the vertical stitch on top. In the other corners, the horizontal stitch is on top. Remaining squares: Upright Cross Stitch. Note that the squares in the vertical plane are crossed with the vertical stitch on top. In the horizontal plane, the first square is crossed with a horizontal stitch on top. In the last square, rows are alternately crossed horizontally and vertically.

Upright Cross Stitch

Also called Straight Cross Stitch

The Upright Cross Stitch is a unit of 2 stitches. The first stitch is a Straight Gobelin over 2 horizontal canvas threads. The second stitch crosses it horizontally over 2 vertical canvas threads. When making a horizontal row a space is skipped between each vertical stitch, which is used by the next row of stitches (101). Stitches can be worked in horizontal, vertical, or diagonal rows (102). The top stitch of the unit can be made either vertically or horizontally (103).

This is a lovely fine grounding stitch. It may be tedious to work in large areas because of all the crossing, but it is well worth trying for its unusual pineapplelike texture. It may be used to simulate pebbles, sand, or shrubbery.

St. George and St. Andrew Cross Stitch

This stitch is a combination of the Upright Cross Stitch (St. George, 104) and the Cross Stitch (St. Andrew, 105). It is easily worked in diagonal rows and shows up best when worked in two colors (106). Put in one color first and then fill in the remaining spaces with the other. The St. George and St. Andrew Cross Stitch is used on the Cross Stitch swatch.

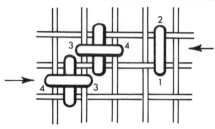

101. *The first half of the stitch is vertical; a horizontal stitch crosses it from left to right. Note the space skipped between each unit. Work rows in alternate directions.*

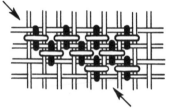

102. *Stitches crossed individually and laid in diagonal rows.*

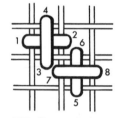

103. *One stitch crossed with a vertical stitch on top, the other with a horizontal stitch on top.*

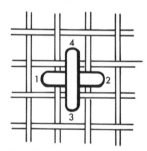

104. *St. George (Upright Cross Stitch).*

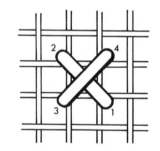

105. *St. Andrew (Cross Stitch).*

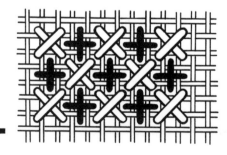

106. *St. George and St. Andrew Stitch.*

Large and Upright Cross Stitch

The large Cross Stitches are set in first over 4 horizontal by 4 vertical canvas threads and crossed individually. The Upright Cross Stitches, taken over 2 horizontal by 2 vertical canvas threads, are then laid between them. Rows are worked in alternate directions (107). The Large and Upright Cross is especially attractive when worked in contrasting colors or textures.

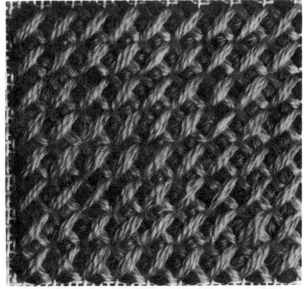

This swatch uses 4-ply Persian for the large crosses and 3-ply Persian for the Upright Crosses. The horizontal rows of Upright Cross are crossed with the horizontal stitch on top; the vertical rows are crossed with the vertical stitch on top. The pattern is made simply by using different colors. The canvas is 12-mesh mono.

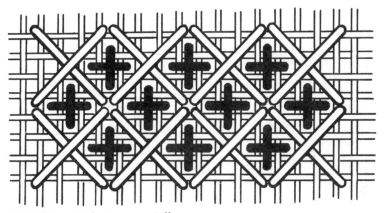

107. This stitch is especially attractive worked in contrasting colors.

Oblong Cross Stitch

Also called Tall Cross Stitch and Double Stitch

The Oblong Cross Stitch (108) is a Cross Stitch made over 2 vertical canvas threads by 3, 4, or 5 horizontal canvas threads. The stitches can be arranged on the canvas in an infinite number of variations and they combine beautifully with many other stitches. The canvas left exposed between stitches can be filled with smaller Cross Stitches (109, 110), Upright Cross Stitches (111) or with Straight Gobelin in contrasting color or texture (112).

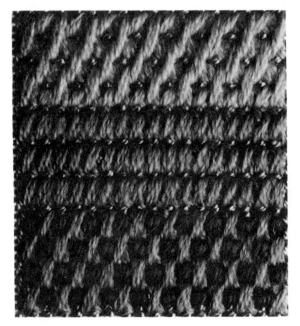

Band 1. This is what diagram 111 looks like when worked.
Band 2. Diagram 112.
Band 3. Diagram 109.
Three-ply Persian and pearl cotton are used on 12-mesh mono.

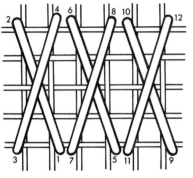

108. A row of Oblong Cross Stitch over 5 horizontal canvas threads.

110. Oblong Cross Stitch over 4 canvas threads. Cross Stitches over 2 threads fill the exposed canvas.

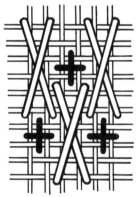

111. Oblong Cross Stitch over 6 horizontal canvas threads, encroaching by 2. Upright Cross fills the exposed canvas.

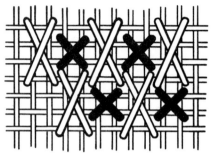

109. Stitches are taken over 4 horizontal canvas threads skipping 2 vertical canvas threads between each unit. The second row of stitches encroaches 1 horizontal canvas thread into the space of the row above. The third row is the same as the first, the fourth the same as the second. Cross Stitches fill open spaces.

112. Rows of Oblong Cross Stitch over 4 canvas threads with Back Stitch between rows and Gobelin Stitch between the crosses.

Crossed Corners Stitch

Also called Rice Stitch and William and Mary Stitch

The Crossed Corners Stitch is a unit of 6 stitches. A large Cross Stitch is made over 4 horizontal by 4 vertical canvas threads (113). The corners are then crossed over 2 mesh in a contrasting color or texture (114, 115). For striking results use a finer or glossier thread to cross the corners.

When working a large area of Crossed Corners it may be easier to work all the Cross Stitches and then cross all corners in diagonal rows traveling up and down the canvas as though doing a large diagonal Tent Stitch (116).

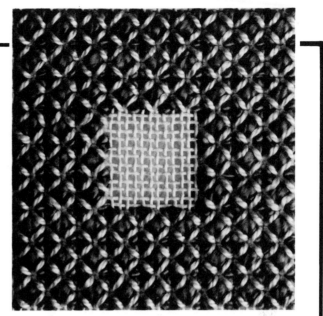

Novelty cotton is used for the large Cross Stitch and pearl cotton for the crossed corners. The square of canvas left blank suggests how this stitch might look if used for a picture frame.

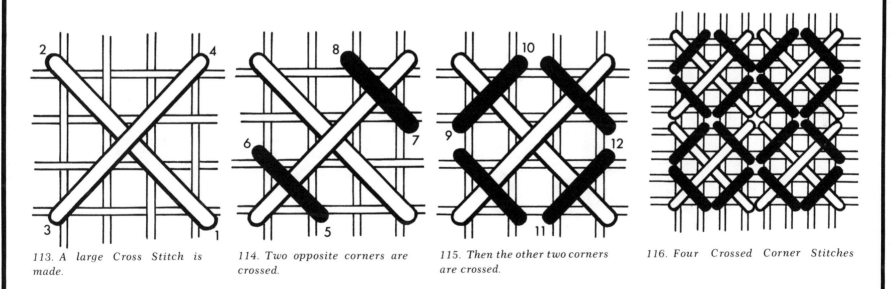

113. *A large Cross Stitch is made.*

114. *Two opposite corners are crossed.*

115. *Then the other two corners are crossed.*

116. *Four Crossed Corner Stitches*

Double Cross Stitch

Also called Double Straight Stitch

Upright Cross Stitches are made over 4 horizontal by 4 vertical canvas threads (117). Cross Stitches are then made over the intersections of the Upright Crosses using 2 horizontal by 2 vertical canvas threads (118). Double Cross Stitches are usually set in staggered rows (119) and are most attractive when worked in two contrasting colors or textures.

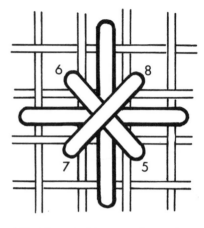

117. Upright Cross Stitch is made first.

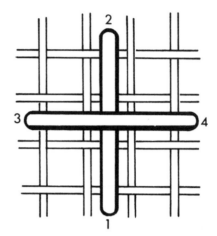

118. If worked in one color each unit is crossed individually.

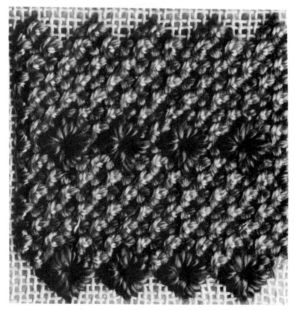

The Upright Cross Stitch is worked in 2-ply Persian, the Cross Stitch in pearl cotton, and the Diamond Eyelet in heavy novelty cotton. For placement of the Diamond Eyelet see diagram 115. The canvas is 12-mesh mono.

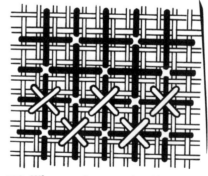

119. When using contrasting threads all Upright Cross Stitches are set in first and then double-crossed with the contrast thread.

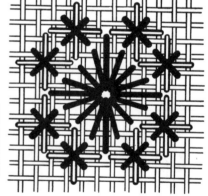

120. Space may be left between stitches for an ornamental stitch such as this Diamond Eyelet taken over 8 horizontal by 8 vertical canvas threads.

Smyrna Stitch

The Smyrna Stitch can be worked over 4 by 4 or 2 by 2 canvas threads. On mono canvas, better coverage is achieved over 2 (123). A large Cross Stitch (121) is made and then crossed, horizontally and vertically, with an Upright Cross Stitch (122).

If a large heavy stitch is desired, try the Leviathan Stitch (diagrams 127–30) which uses all canvas threads around the perimeter of the 4-by-4 canvas thread unit.

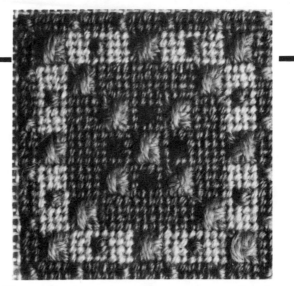

The smaller decorative stitches are Smyrna Stitches taken over 2 canvas threads. The larger decorative stitches are Leviathan Stitches. The background is Tent Stitch. All stitches are worked in 2-ply Persian on 12-mesh mono.

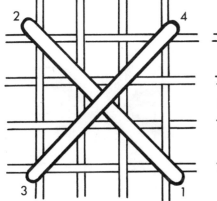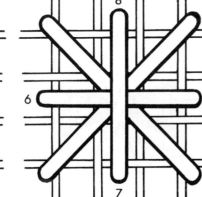

123. Smyrna Stitch over 2 horizontal by 2 vertical canvas threads. Note that all canvas threads are covered.

121 and 122. Smyrna Stitch over 4 horizontal by 4 vertical canvas threads. Note that some canvas may be exposed.

97

Triple Cross Stitch

The Triple Cross Stitch is worked in an area of 3 horizontal by 3 vertical canvas threads. An Oblong Cross Stitch is made over 1 horizontal by 3 vertical canvas threads (124). It is then crossed with another Oblong Cross over 3 horizontal by 1 vertical canvas thread (125). Finally it is crossed with a Cross Stitch over 3 horizontal by 3 vertical canvas threads (126). Because most needlepoint stitches are worked over an even number of canvas threads, the Triple Cross is a handy stitch to have in your stitch repertoire.

All the medium-size stitches are Triple Cross. The small stitches are Smyrna and the 4 large stitches are Leviathan. The background is Tent Stitch. All stitches are worked on 2-ply Persian on 12-mesh mono.

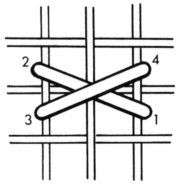

124. *The first cross is laid on its side.*

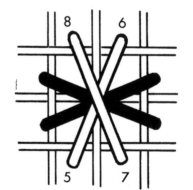

125. *The second cross is vertical.*

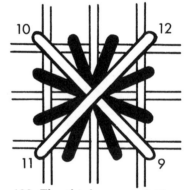

126. *The third cross is laid on top.*

Leviathan Stitch

A large Cross Stitch is worked over 4 horizontal by 4 vertical canvas threads (127). Each arm of the stitch is then crossed systematically as shown in diagrams 128 and 129. An Upright Cross Stitch is then made using the remaining mesh openings; the vertical stitch is taken last (130).

I prefer using a Leviathan to a Smyrna when filling an area of 4 horizontal by 4 vertical canvas threads because the Leviathan covers all canvas threads. See the Triple Cross Stitch swatch for samples of Leviathan Stitch.

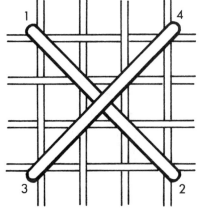

127. Note that the Cross Stitch is started at the upper left instead of the lower right; an exception to the rule.

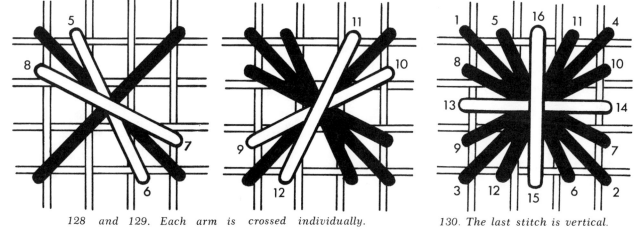

128 and 129. Each arm is crossed individually.

130. The last stitch is vertical.

Long-armed Cross Stitch

Also called Long-legged Cross Stitch

The Long-armed Cross Stitch is worked in horizontal rows back and forth across the canvas. It always starts with a Cross Stitch, the first arm of which heads in the direction of the row. Thus, if you are working from left to right, the first half of the Cross Stitch would slant from lower left to upper right (131). The next stitch is the long arm. It comes out the same opening as the first stitch and is taken over 4 vertical canvas threads. The needle then goes down under 2 threads (132), crosses back over 2 threads, and goes down under 2 threads (133). The whole unit is then repeated starting with a long arm at 9 in diagram 134.

This may sound complicated but it is really a simple stitch once mastered. The second row travels from the opposite direction, from right to left. It starts with a Cross Stitch, but the first arm now slants from lower right to upper left (135).

Many of the needlepoint rugs that come from Portugal are made with this stitch. It looks very much like the Greek Stitch, but the Greek Stitch makes small horizontal stitches on the back of the canvas, and the Long-armed Cross makes vertical stitches.

You can make mini Long-armed Cross Stitches on penelope by treating each double set of threads as 2 mono canvas threads. Because this stitch goes over units of 2 canvas threads there is no need to prick apart the vertical canvas threads.

The first 4 rows are Long-armed Cross Stitches traveling from left to right and returning from right to left. The remaining rows alternate Long-armed Cross worked from left to right and Tent Stitch worked from right to left. This makes an interesting pattern and may be easier for some. To work the Long-armed Cross vertically, give the canvas a quarter turn.

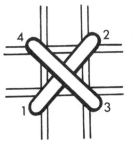

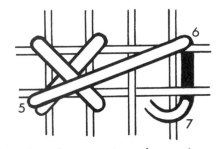

131. *Long-armed Cross Stitch starts with a Cross Stitch.*

132. *A long arm is made over 4 vertical canvas threads.*

133. *The long arm is crossed with a short stitch.*

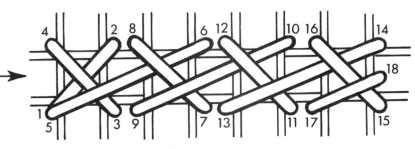

134. *Completed row of Long-armed Cross Stitch worked from left to right. Note that the row ends with a compensating stitch to cover the vertical canvas thread that would otherwise be exposed.*

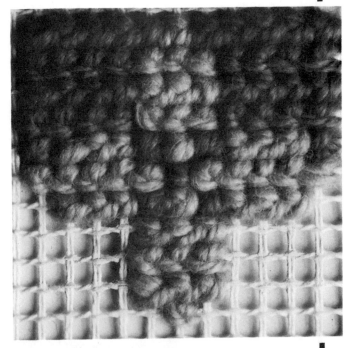

Using Paternayan rug wool on 3½-mesh penelope you can work up a rug in relatively short time. The double vertical canvas threads are counted as 2 threads when working a Cross or Long-armed Cross Stitch.

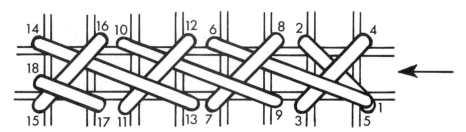

135. *Completed row worked from right to left. The same compensating stitch is taken at the other side.*

Greek Stitch

This stitch, which starts at the top, is another exception to the rule that all stitches must start at the base of the stitch. A Cross Stitch is made (136) and then a long arm is taken from the same mesh opening as the top of the first stitch and crosses over 4 vertical canvas threads. The needle is held in a horizontal position and goes back under 2 vertical canvas threads (137), crosses over 2 threads, and goes back under 2 canvas threads (138). The whole unit is then repeated, starting with the long arm (139). Stitches are worked in horizontal rows from left to right. The work is turned upside down at the end of each row so that the next row can be worked in the same direction. Each row starts with a Cross Stitch and ends with a compensating stitch to cover the vertical canvas thread that would otherwise be exposed.

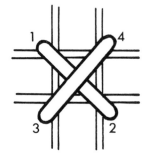

136. A Cross Stitch is made.

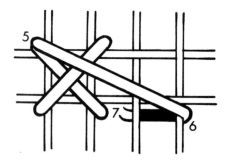

137. A long arm is made.

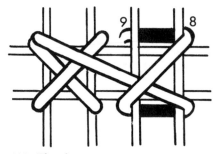

138. The long arm is crossed and the needle is in position for another long arm.

When changing colors within a pattern you can either close the row, as shown in diagram 139, or have the stitches flow into one another by making part of the stitch in one color and completing it with the next, as shown here. The Greek Stitch is worked in 2-ply Persian on 12-mesh mono.

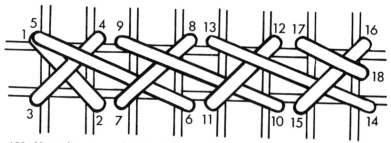

139. Note the row is closed with a short stitch at the end. Work is turned to start next row.

Plait Stitch

Also called Spanish Stitch

This stitch is very similar to the Long-armed Cross Stitch: it travels ahead with a long diagonal arm and crosses back with a shorter stitch. The Plait Stitch travels more slowly because the stitches overlap one another. A Cross Stitch is made and a rhythm of back 1 canvas thread, forward 2 is established. The stitch can be worked over 2, 3, 4, or 5 horizontal canvas threads. Worked through a folded edge of canvas, it makes a finished, bound edge for a belt or a rug.

Gobelin Plait Stitch

A row of Slanting Gobelin Stitches is made over 2 horizontal by 2 vertical canvas threads. The needle is taken under 2 horizontal canvas threads and is brought up through the canvas at the base of the next stitch. In this way a space is skipped between each stitch. A second row travels in the opposite direction, crossing the base of stitches of the previous row and going into the spaces between the stitches. The third row travels in the direction of the first and crosses the stitches in the second row.

Upper: *Rows of Gobelin Plait Stitch are shown worked in bands of different colors.*
Lower: *A Plait Stitch is worked over 5 horizontal canvas threads to make a frame with mitered corners. The bottom row of stitches is taken over 2 canvas threads and would make an excellent edging for a belt.*
Three-ply Persian is used on 12-mesh mono.

  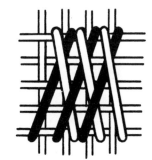  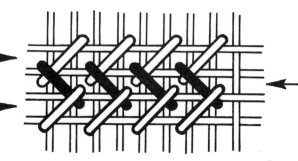

140. Cross Stitch, back 1 canvas thread.

141. Forward 2 canvas threads.

142. Back 1, forward 2, back 1, forward 2.

143. Plait Stitch over 2 horizontal canvas threads.

144. First row travels from left to right (forward 2 and over 2 canvas threads). Second row returns from right to left, into the first row. Third row travels as first, into second row.

Tied and Looped Stitches

Shell Stitch
Tied Oblong Cross Stitch
Double and Tie Stitch
French Stitch
Rococo Stitch
Web Stitch
Knotted Stitch
Fishbone Stitch
Chain Stitch
Turkey Knot Stitch
Velvet Stitch
Surrey Stitch

Shell Stitch

The Shell Stitch is made of 4 Straight Gobelin Stitches taken over 4 or 6 horizontal canvas threads. The stitches are tied down with a horizontal stitch that comes out to the left of the center vertical canvas thread, wraps around the 4 stitches, and goes through the opening to the right of the center vertical canvas thread (145). Upright Cross Stitches are used to cover exposed canvas between stitches and Back Stitches are worked between rows (147).

To connect the "sheaves," a coiling thread may be added to link the center stitches together (148).

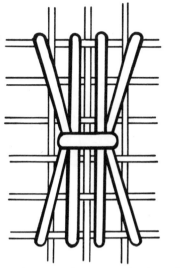

145. Note the point of exit and entry of the center horizontal stitch.

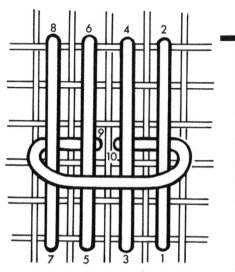

146. Single Shell Stitch over 6 canvas threads.

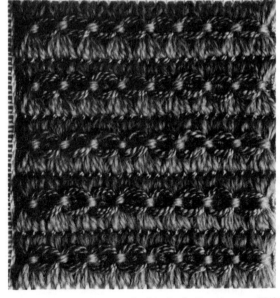

The Shell Stitch is worked in 2-ply Persian on 10/20-mesh penelope. The Back Stitch between the rows and the coils uses pearl cotton; the Upright Cross Stitch is done in 7-ply French silk.

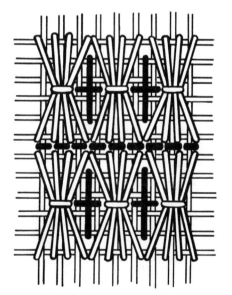

147. Upright Cross Stitch and Back Stitch cover exposed canvas threads.

148. A coil is worked from right to left, coiling from the center of the coil out, linking the Back Stitches.

Tied Oblong Cross Stitch

Oblong Cross Stitches are made over 4 or 6 horizontal canvas threads. Back Stitches are then taken over the central mesh openings to tie them down (149). The Back Stitch is usually worked in a contrasting color. This stitch is particularly striking over 6 canvas threads and tied down with 3 Back Stitches (150).

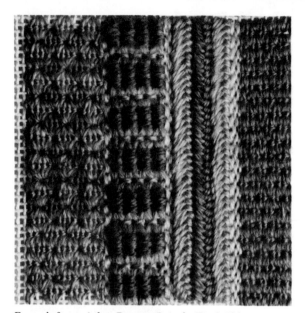

From left to right: Rococo Stitch, Tied Oblong Cross Stitch, Fishbone Stitch, French Stitch. Staggered Back Stitches are taken between each column.
The Tied Oblong Cross is taken over 6 horizontal canvas threads using 2-ply Persian. It is tied 3 times in contrasting colors. The Back Stitch between the rows is taken over 2 canvas threads instead of 1. The canvas is 14-mesh mono.
The French Stitch is made with 1-ply Persian. It has a rough, textured, uneven appearance. Because of this effect, it is used for the tree trunk in the Genesis Sampler on pages 2–3 of photo insert.
The Fishbone Stitch is worked in 2-ply Persian. The stitch itself creates a handsome vertical stripe.

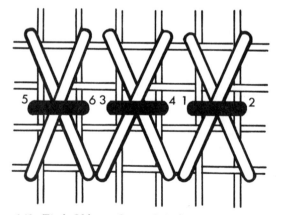

149. Tied Oblong Cross Stitch over 4 horizontal canvas threads, tied down once at the cross.

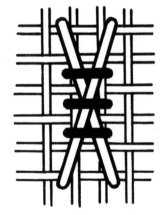

150. Tied Oblong Cross Stitch over 6 horizontal canvas threads, tied 3 times.

Double and Tie Stitch

Also called Paris Stitch

The Double and Tie Stitch is made of 2 Straight Gobelin Stitches taken over 4 horizontal canvas threads and between 2 vertical canvas threads (151). The 2 stitches are tied down in the center with a stitch taken over the 2 central vertical canvas threads (152). This is an excellent rug stitch. It works very comfortably in diagonal rows (153).

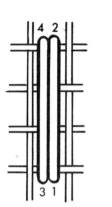

151. Two stitches are taken in 1 mesh opening.

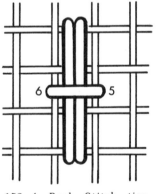

152. A Back Stitch ties the stitches down.

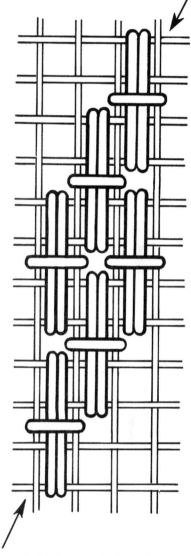

153. Double and Tie Stitch worked in diagonal rows Complete each unit before going on to the next stitch.

This 5-mesh penelope is worked with rug wool. The Double and Tie Stitch is worked in diagonal rows, each row in a different color. A bold contemporary rug could be worked very quickly in this stitch. Slant diagonal rows in opposite directions for a stunning zigzag pattern.

French Stitch

The French Stitch starts with a Straight Gobelin Stitch taken over 4 horizontal canvas threads. It is tied down in the center to the vertical canvas thread to the left of the stitch (154). A second Straight Gobelin is made over the same 4 canvas threads and is tied down to the vertical canvas thread to the right of the stitch (155). Both tieing stitches are taken from the outside of the stitch into the center of the stitch. Stitches are worked in diagonal rows (156). This is a slow-moving stitch and requires special care and skill. See the Tied Oblong Cross Stitch swatch for the French Stitch in use.

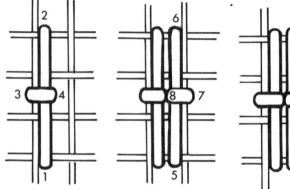

154. *The center stitch ties a Straight Gobelin to a vertical canvas thread at the left.*

155. *A second Gobelin is tied to the vertical canvas thread at the right.*

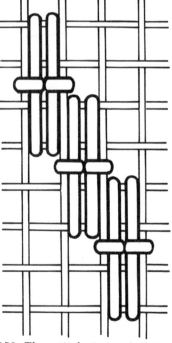

156. *The stitch is worked in diagonal rows. Complete each unit before going on to the next stitch.*

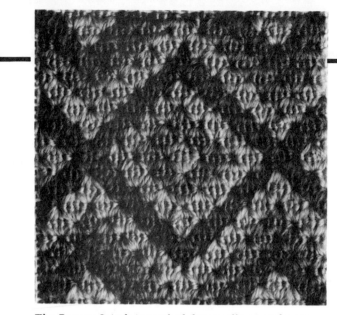

The Rococo Stitch is worked diagonally to make zig-zags and diamonds. Notice how the pattern is established by the use of a few different colors. Two-ply Persian is used on 12-mesh mono. See the Tied Oblong Cross Stitch swatch for Rococo worked in 2-ply Persian on 14-mesh mono.

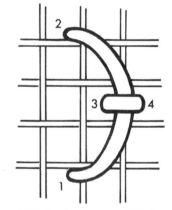

157. *Each Rococo Stitch unit uses 4 horizontal by 4 vertical canvas threads. The first Straight Gobelin Stitch is made and tied to the first vertical canvas thread.*

Rococo Stitch

This is an unusual stitch. Do not be intimidated by it; it is really quite simple to master. Each unit uses 4 horizontal by 4 vertical canvas threads. The stitch is made of 4 Straight Gobelin Stitches. Each stitch comes out the same mesh opening at the base of the unit and goes in the same mesh opening at the top. Each of the 4 stitches is tied down as it is made to the center of a different vertical canvas thread (157–160). The Rococo Stitch is a very unique, lacy-looking stitch that can be used as grounding. Work it in horizontal or diagonal rows (161).

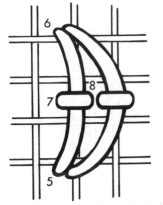

158. The second Gobelin is made and tied to the second vertical canvas thread.

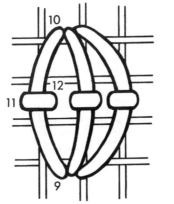

159. The third Gobelin is tied to the third vertical canvas thread.

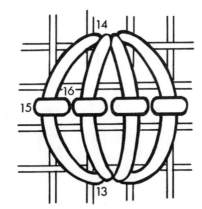

160. The fourth Gobelin is tied to the last vertical canvas thread. Note the first 2 Straight Gobelin Stitches fan to the right since they are tied to the right. The last 2 fan to the left because they are tied to the left.

161. Note that 4 units of Rococo Stitch share the same mesh opening and create an eyelet effect.

Web Stitch

The Web Stitch starts in an upper left position with a Tent Stitch. Long diagonal stitches are taken and tied down as they are made with Reversed Tent Stitches, either at every horizontal canvas thread (164) or at every other (163). The diagonal stitches grow 1 canvas thread larger as they move to the next mesh opening at the side and the top (162). This stitch looks prettiest in silk. I suggest using it only in small areas as it can be tedious.

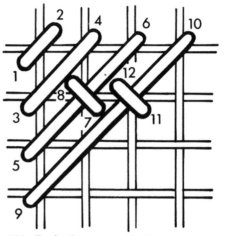

162. Each diagonal stitch, beginning with the third, is tied down as it is made.

This checkerboard design is created by working Web Stitch in even squares. Every other square is worked with the canvas held with the top at the side to change the direction of the stitch. Seven-ply French silk is used on 12-mesh mono.

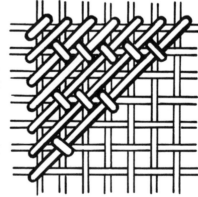

163. Web Stitch tied down to every other horizontal canvas thread.

164. Web Stitch tied down to every horizontal canvas thread.

Knotted Stitch

A Slanting Gobelin Stitch is taken over 3 horizontal by 1 vertical canvas thread. It is tied down as it is made with a Reversed Tent Stitch taken over the center mesh (165). Stitches are worked in horizontal rows that travel in alternate directions. Each row begins 2 canvas threads beneath the previous row and encroaches 1 canvas thread into the row above (166).

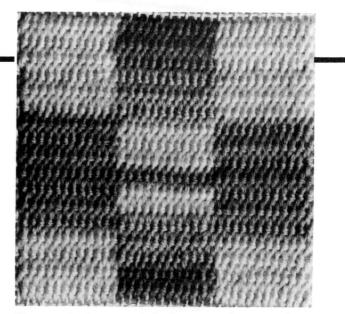

The use of color creates the design on this 12-mesh mono canvas. The Knotted Stitch is worked in 2-ply Persian.

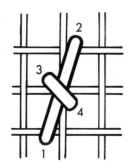

165. *Each stitch is tied down individually.*

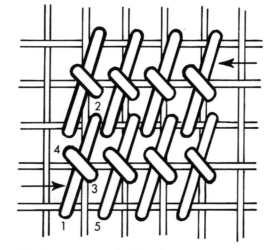

166. *Rows are worked in alternate directions. Note how the second row encroaches on the first.*

Fishbone Stitch

A Slanting Gobelin Stitch is made over 3 horizontal by 3 vertical canvas threads and tied down with a Reversed Tent Stitch at the top of each stitch (167). Stitches are worked in a vertical row using consecutive mesh openings. The second row is made with the long stitches slanting in the opposite direction, tied down at the base (168). Rows alternate the direction of the long stitch. The third row is the same as the first, the fourth row is the same as the second (169). See the Tied Oblong Cross Stitch swatch for the Fishbone Stitch in use.

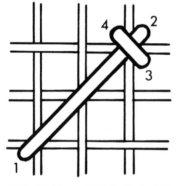

167. *Fishbone Stitch tied at the top.*

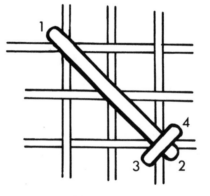

168. *Fishbone Stitch slanting in the opposite direction and tied at the base.*

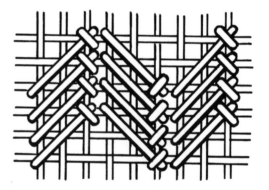

169. *Fishbone Stitch worked vertically; each row slants in an alternate direction.*

Chain Stitch

This is the same Chain Stitch used in fabric embroidery. It is worked in vertical rows from the top down. For a regular, even appearance, end each row at its base and begin the next row anew. To make a horizontal row, give the canvas a quarter turn so that the top is at the side; the row is then worked vertically. The Chain Stitch must be worked over 2 horizontal and between 2 vertical canvas threads on mono canvas. It is easily worked on penelope canvas using only the large mesh openings. The Chain Stitch is an excellent grounding stitch that resembles knitting.

This swatch is worked in 2-ply Persian on 12-mesh mono. The log cabin design is worked by changing the direction of the stitch. In the center the braided-rug effect is accomplished by stitching a continuous chain. The Chain Stitch is used for the horse in the Genesis Sampler on pages 2–3 of photo insert.

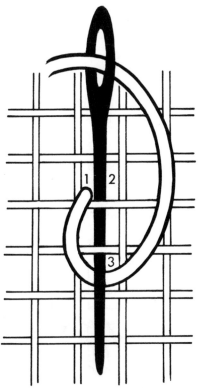

170. After coming out a mesh opening, the needle goes back into the same opening and comes out under 2 horizontal canvas threads, looping the yarn under its pointed end.

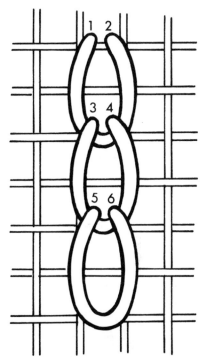

171. When the needle is drawn it catches the loop and the first chain is made. Each stitch is tied down by the stitch that follows it.

Turkey Knot Stitch

Also called Ghiordes Knot and Turkey Knot Tufting

This is the easiest of three looped stitches. It can be used to make a pile rug, to fringe a rug, or to edge a pillow. All rows are worked horizontally from left to right. If a vertical row is needed, as for the sides of a pillow, the canvas is given a quarter turn and the row is continued from left to right. Work the outermost row first so that the pile does not cover the unworked area, progressing row by row from the bottom to the top. A row or two of canvas may be left bare between rows of stitches depending on the fullness desired.

Note that the tail end of the yarn is on the front of the canvas when starting a row and that the stitch starts by going in at 1, an exception to the rule. Leaving about an inch of yarn on the front, the needle goes in a mesh opening and comes out through the next opening to the left. A horizontal straight stitch is made over 2 vertical canvas threads and the needle comes out the original mesh opening (172).

The thumb is now used to hold the yarn to the desired length of the loop, and a horizontal straight stitch is made to tighten it (173). When done, the loops may be left uncut (174) or clipped. Turkey Knot works easily on the double threads of penelope canvas, but can be used on mono canvas over the 2 vertical canvas threads as shown in the diagrams.

The Turkey Knot is worked in 2-ply Persian on 14-mesh mono. Note that the fringe is shaded, each row using a different value of the same color. A row of canvas is skipped between rows.

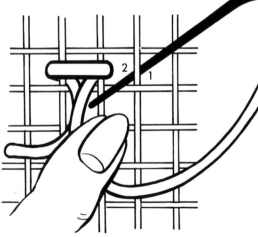

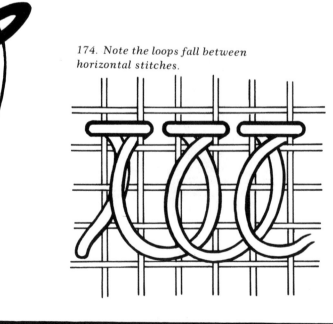

174. *Note the loops fall between horizontal stitches.*

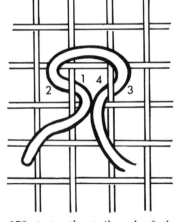

172. *Note the tail end of the yarn is on the front of the canvas.*

173. *Where you hold your thumb on the yarn determines the size of the loop.*

Velvet Stitch

This is another looped stitch used for pile rugs, fringe, or for a raised texture. Like the Turkey Knot, work from left to right and from the last row to the first. One or two rows may be left between rows of stitches if less fullness is desired. When possible use long double-length strands of yarn for all looped stitches as they use a lot of wool, and frequent ending and starting is a nuisance.

The Velvet Stitch is worked in an area of 2 horizontal by 2 vertical canvas threads on mono canvas, and 1 or 2 sets of horizontal and vertical canvas threads on penelope. Start by making a Half Cross Stitch (175). Bring the needle up through the canvas at the base of this stitch and, using the thumb, hold the yarn to the length you want the loop. The needle now goes into the top of the original stitch and comes out directly under 2 canvas threads (176). Holding the loop to the left of the needle, close the stitch as you would the Cross Stitch, and come out the next vacant lower left mesh opening (177).

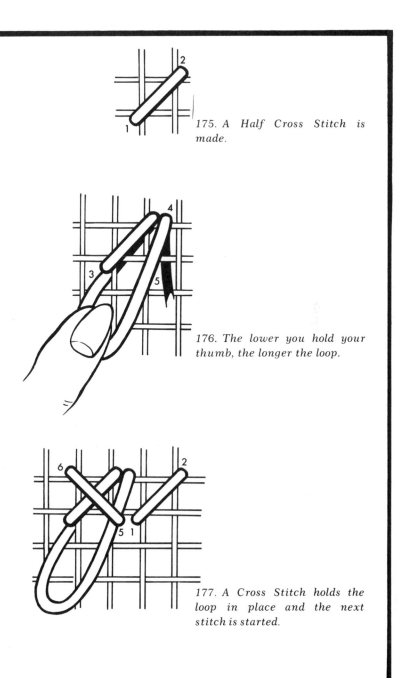

175. A Half Cross Stitch is made.

176. The lower you hold your thumb, the longer the loop.

177. A Cross Stitch holds the loop in place and the next stitch is started.

Two bands of Velvet Stitch are worked in 3-ply Persian on 12-mesh mono. Top: Three rows of cut Velvet Stitch. Bottom: Two rows of uncut Velvet Stitch with a row of Tied Oblong Cross Stitch added for decorative effect.

Surrey Stitch

The Surrey Stitch must be worked from left to right and from the last row to the first, like all looped stitches. If a vertical row is desired, as for the sides of a pillow, the canvas is given a quarter turn and the work is continued from left to right. On mono canvas an area of 2 horizontal by 2 vertical canvas threads are used; on penelope 1 set of vertical and horizontal canvas threads can be used.

Note that the tail end of the thread is on the front of the canvas. The stitch starts by going in at 1. It comes out directly under 2 canvas threads (178).

The tail end of the yarn is now flipped down and held by the thumb to the left and just below the work. The other end of the yarn is flipped up, above and over the work. The needle is held horizontally and goes under the 2 vertical canvas threads to the right of the first mesh opening (179). Draw the needle through and the first knot is made (180).

Hold the yarn with the thumb to establish the length of the loop—a thumb's width will do at first—and with the needle in a vertical position, go into the third mesh opening and come out under 2 horizontal canvas threads (165). The tip of the needle should be on top of the loop you are holding with your thumb (181). The yarn is then flipped up and above, and another knot is made.

If small, even loops are desired, a knitting needle may be used to hold a row of loops evenly in place.

Three rows of Surrey Stitch are worked from the bottom edge up, clipped and shaded from dark to light. On top there are a few Surrey Stitches left uncut. Two-ply Persian is worked on 12-mesh mono.

116

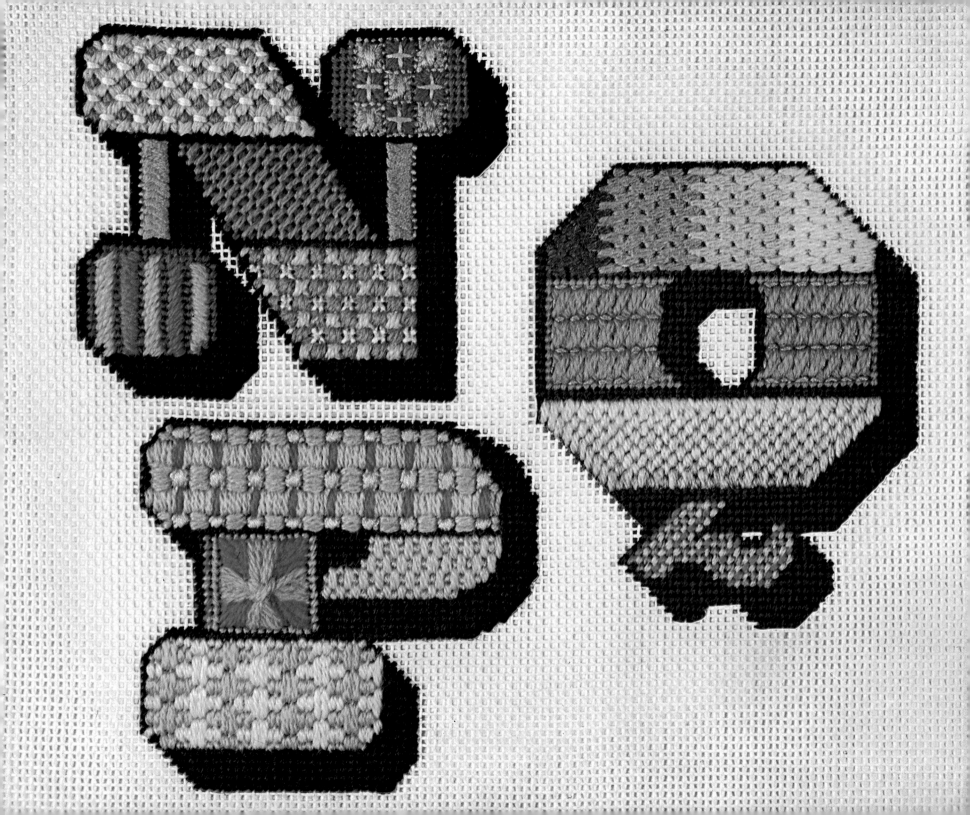

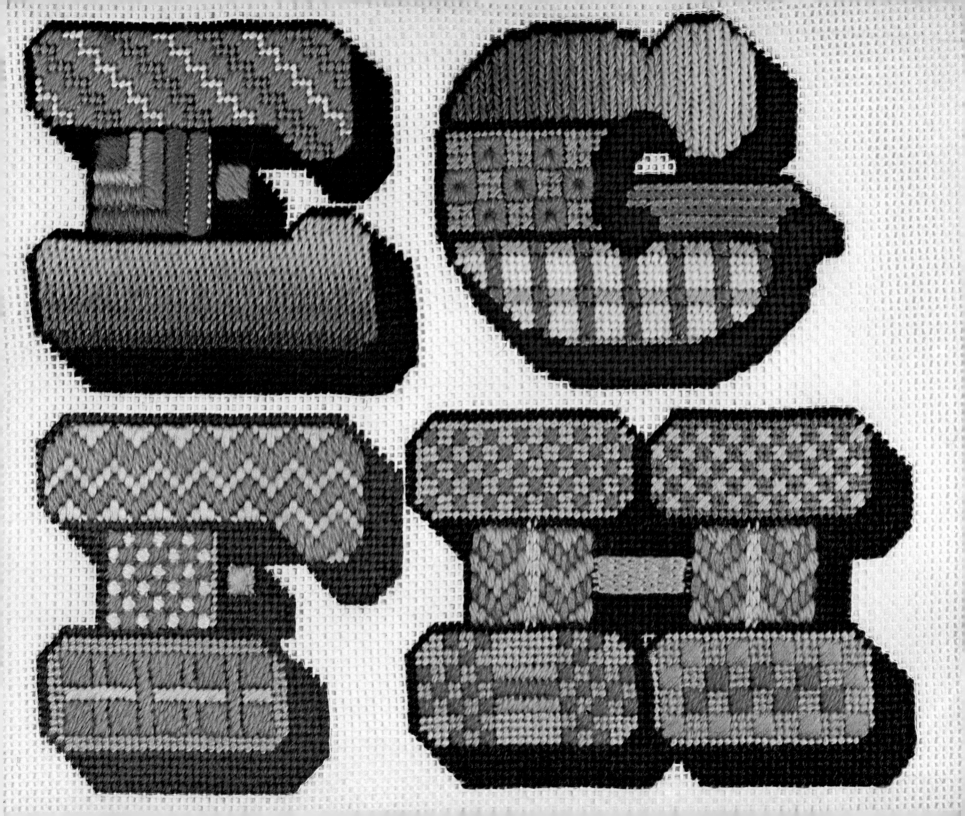

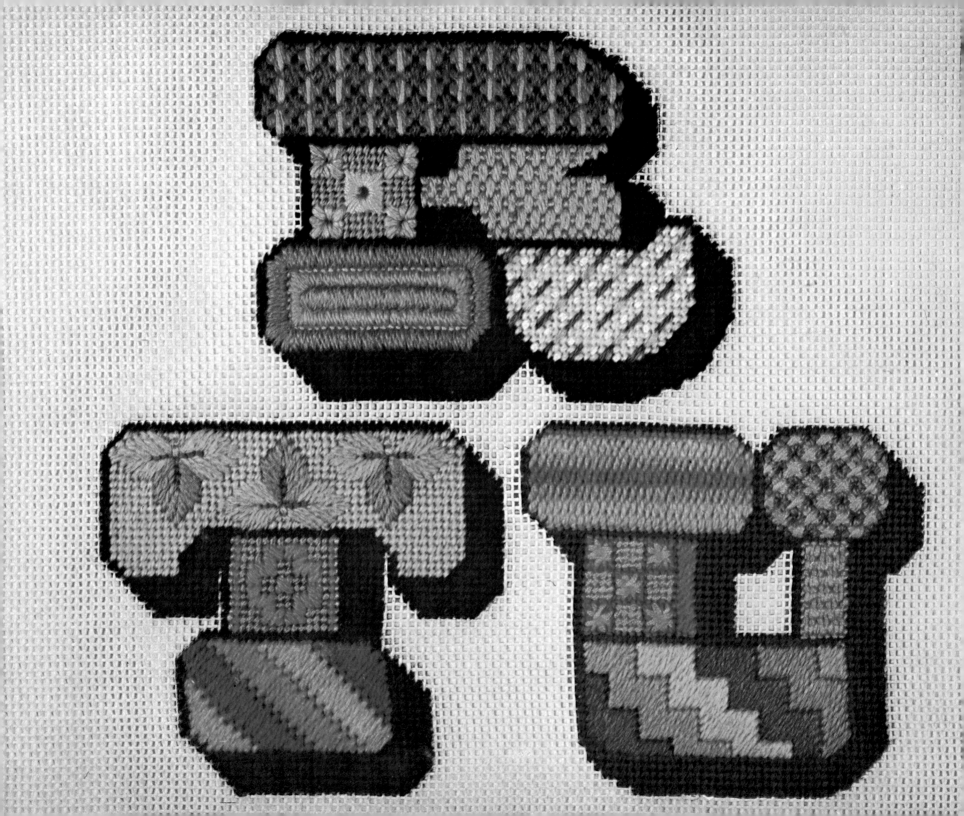

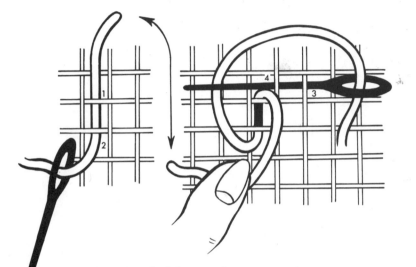

178. *The tail end of the yarn is on the front of the canvas.*

179. *The tip of the needle comes out over the flipped-up yarn.*

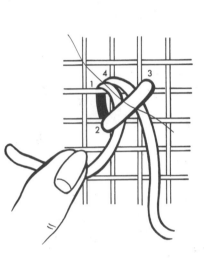

180. *The first knot is made without a loop.*

181. *The loop is made between the stitches.*

The Alphabet Sampler

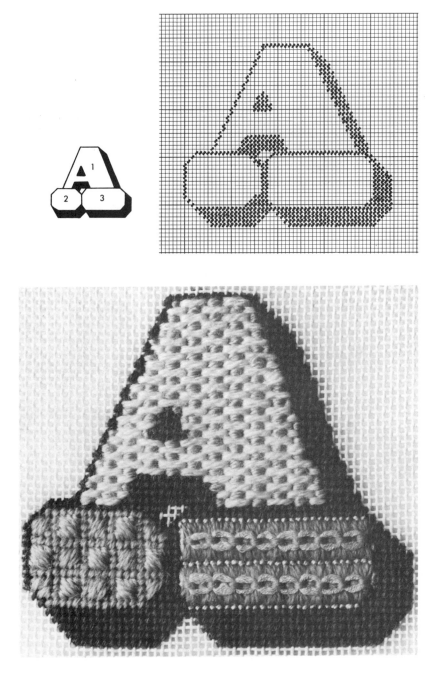

Letter A

1. Parisian Stitch.
2. Scottish Stitch; Flat Stitch portion worked in alternate directions.
3. Shell Stitch.

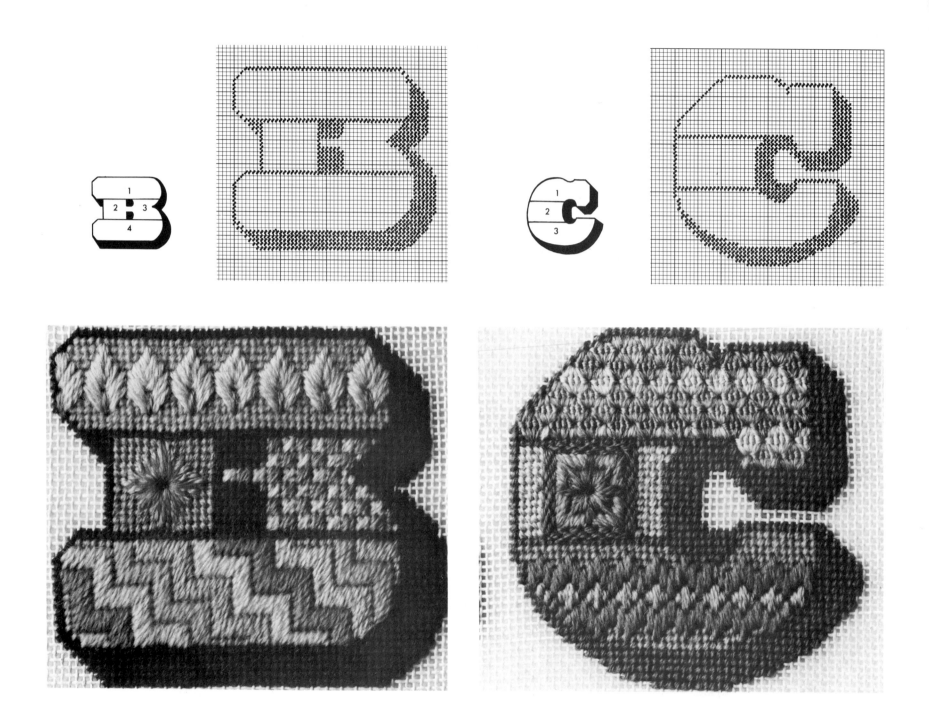

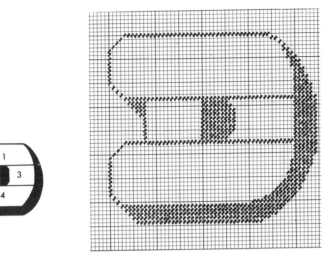

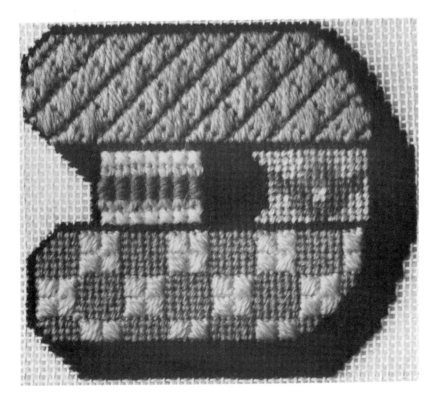

Letter B

1. Leaf Stitch on Tent Stitch ground.
2. Diamond Eyelet Stitch on Tent Stitch ground.
3. Mosaic Stitch worked in boxes.
4. Byzantine Stitch.

Letter C

1. Rococo Stitch.
2. Eyelet Stitch in center, outlined with Slanting Gobelin and Back Stitch, each worked in two directions, on Tent Stitch ground, also worked in two directions. Eyelet is overstitched on completion.
3. Hungarian Ground.

Letter D

1. Hungarian Diamond back-stitched in diagonal rows.
2. Tied Oblong Cross Stitch in center outlined with Back Stitch; Cross Stitch at top and bottom.
3. Tent Stitch.
4. Cushion Stitch outlined with Back Stitch, alternating with boxes of Tent.

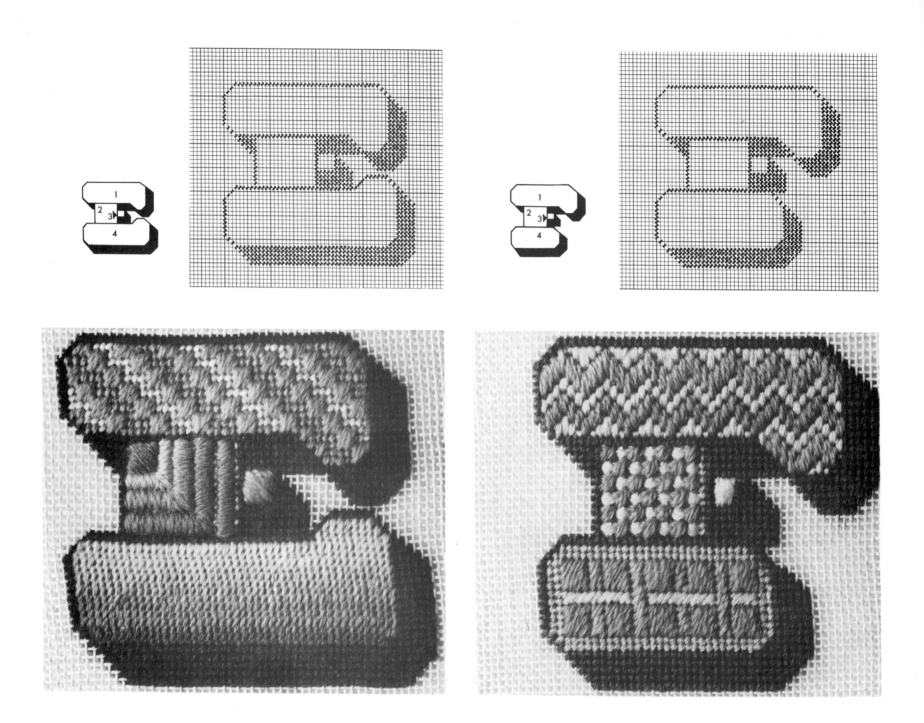

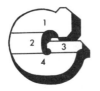

Letter E

1. Moorish Stitch.
2. Flat Stitch in corner (direction of stitch reversed). Straight Gobelin Stitch worked in two directions.
3. Flat Stitch (direction of stitch reversed).
4. Encroaching Gobelin Stitch with blending.

Letter F

1. Wave Stitch.
2. St. George and St. Andrew Cross Stitch; single row of vertical Tent Stitch.
3. Leviathan Stitch.
4. Slanting Gobelin Stitch outlining Flat Stitch panes.

Letter G

1. Kalem Stitch in vertical rows with blending.
2. Eyelet Stitch alternating with boxes of Mosaic Stitch; row of horizontal Tent Stitch at top.
3. Kalem Stitch in horizontal rows.
4. Vertical and horizontal Cashmere Stitch with Smyrna Stitch at intersections; panes of Tent Stitch.

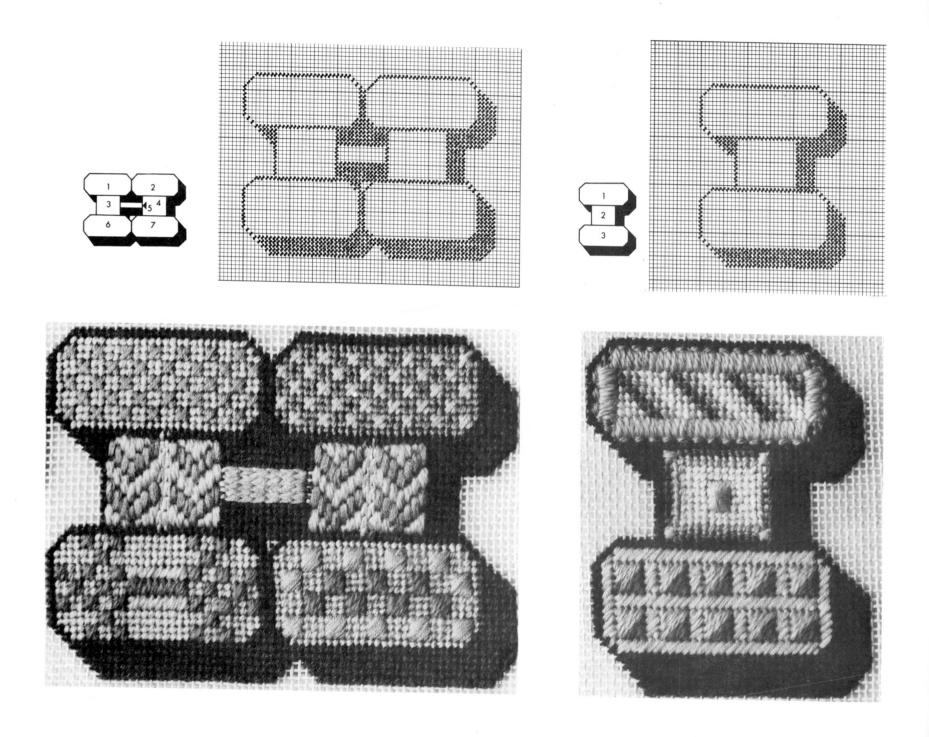

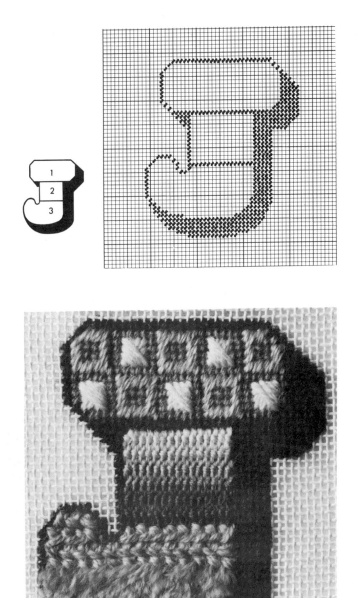

Letter H

1. Small Chequer Stitch partially outlined with Tent Stitch.
2. Small Chequer Stitch partially outlined with Tent Stitch.
3. Wave Stitch parted in middle by vertical Chain Stitch.
4. Wave Stitch parted in middle by vertical Chain Stitch.
5. Horizontal Chain Stitch.
6. Slanting Gobelin Stitch in center with Small Chequer Stitch at sides; Tent Stitch ground.
7. Large Chequer Stitch with Tent Stitch outline.

Letter I

1. Reversed Tent Stitch striping; Straight Gobelin Stitch worked in two directions for border; Tent Stitch corners; Back Stitch outline.
2. Triple Cross Stitch in center on Tent Stitch ground, outlined with Reversed Tent Stitch and Back Stitch; Smyrna Stitch corners.
3. Shaded Flat Stitch outlined with vertical and horizontal Slanting Gobelin Stitch.

Letter J

1. Alternate squares of Tent Stitch outlined with Slanting Gobelin and Flat Stitch outlined with Tent Stitch. The Flat Stitch square is made and then the unit is reworked in opposite direction.
2. Shaded Knotted Stitch.
3. Long-armed Cross Stitch.

127

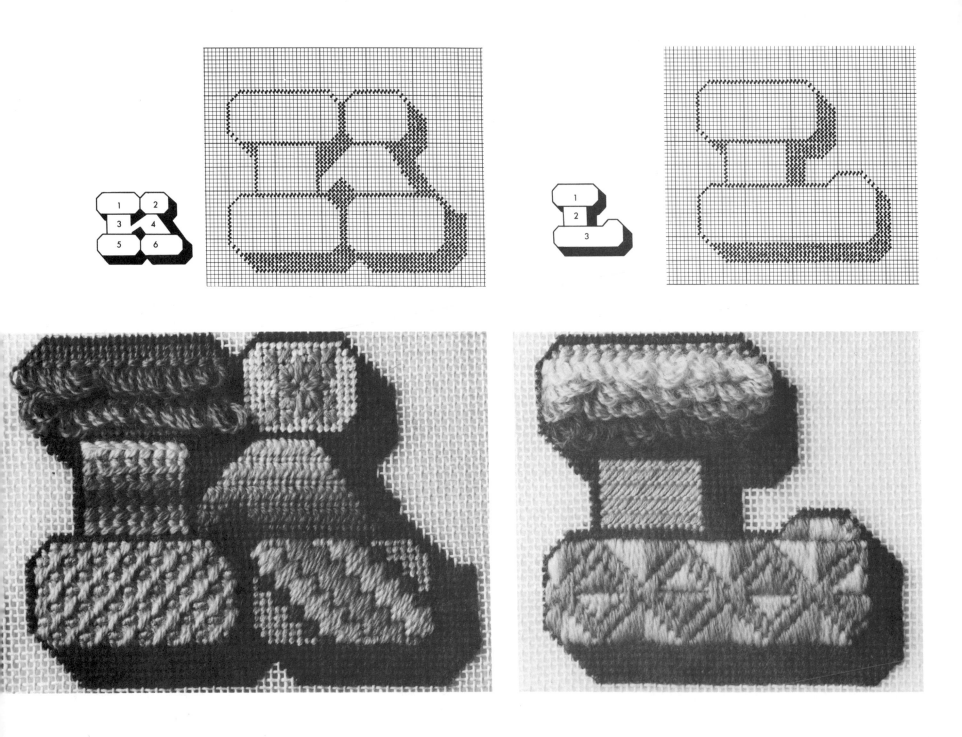

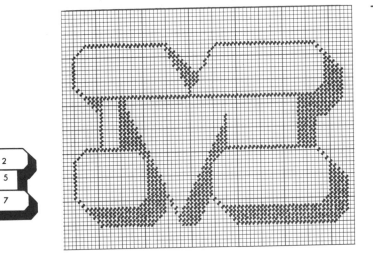

Letter K

1. Turkey Knot on Tent Stitch ground.
2. From center out: Tent Stitch, Hungarian Stitch, and Mosaic Stitch on Tent Stitch ground.
3. Greek Stitch.
4. Alternate rows of Plait and Tent Stitch.
5. Oblong Cross Stitch alternating with Smyrna Stitch (not crossed horizontally).
6. Continuous Flat Stitch outlined with Mosaic Stitch on Tent Stitch ground.

Letter L

1. Surrey Stitch fringe with row of Long-armed Cross Stitch at top and Tent Stitch at bottom.
2. Web Stitch.
3. Bargello.

Letter M

1. Large and Upright Cross Stitch, four Back Stitches at intersections.
2. Shaded Gobelin Plait Stitch.
3. Slanting Gobelin Stitch in vertical rows.
4. Bargello, 4.2 step; alternate rows 2.2 step.
5. Fishbone Stitch.
6. Continuous Cashmere Stitch (direction reversed).
7. Continuous Cashmere Stitch.

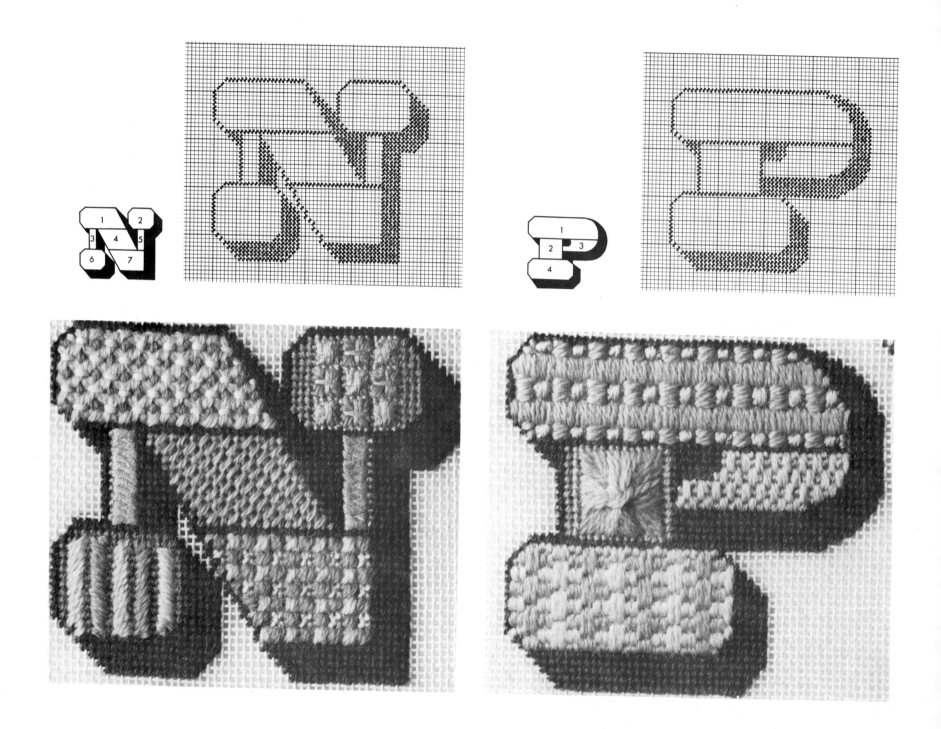

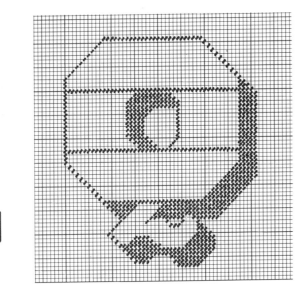

Letter N

1. Oblong Cross Stitch tied down with Back Stitch; Upright Cross Stitch in between.
2. Alternate boxes of Leviathan and Mosaic Stitch overstitched with Upright Cross; Back Stitch around boxes, Tent and Reversed Tent Stitch at sides.
3. Plait Stitch.
4. Continuous Mosaic Stitch.
5. Plait Stitch.
6. Stem Stitch with Tent Stitch at top and sides.
7. Cross Stitch with Smyrna Stitch at regular intervals.

Letter O

Omit tail of Q to make O.

Letter P

1. Narrow stripes: horizontal Straight Gobelin and Smyrna Stitches. Wider stripes: vertical Straight Gobelin.
2. Large two-color Leviathan Stitch with Cross Stitch at center; outlined with Tent Stitch.
3. Parisian Stitch.
4. Hungarian Stitch.

Letter Q

1. Shaded horizontal Brick Stitch.
2. Straight Gobelin Stitch between rows of Oblong Cross Stitch; Back Stitch between rows.
3. Same as 2.
4. Blended vertical Brick Stitch.
5. Tent Stitch.

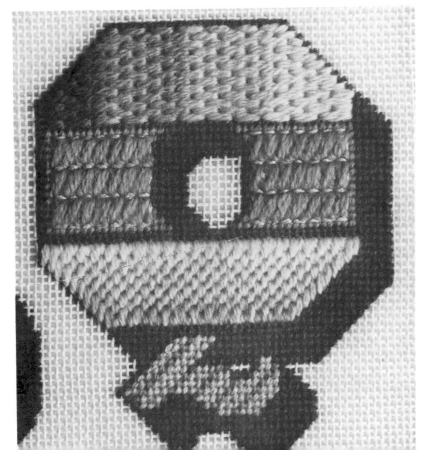

131

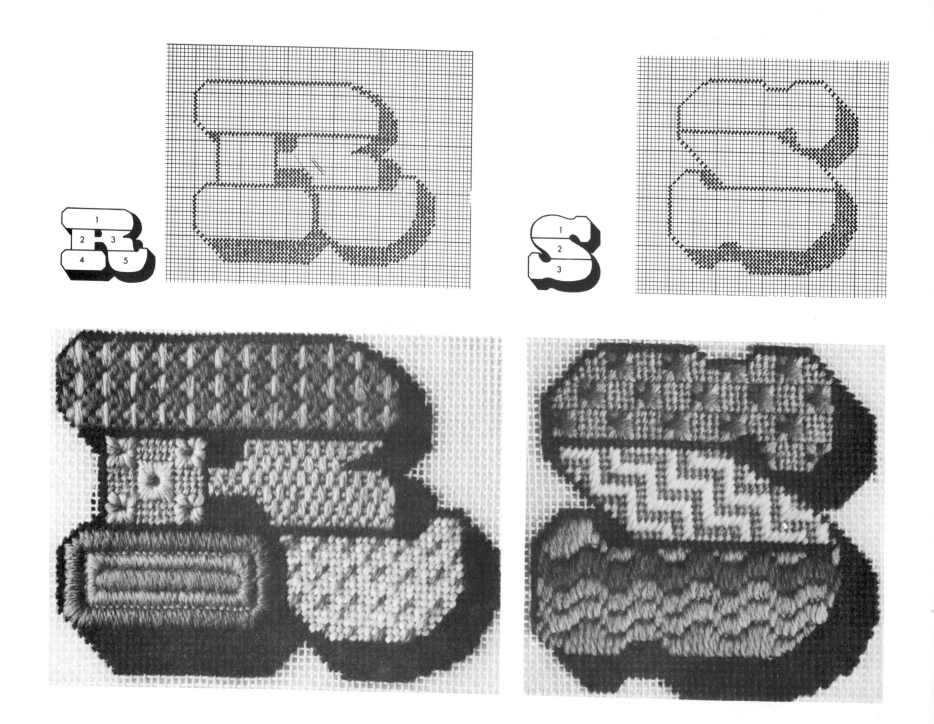

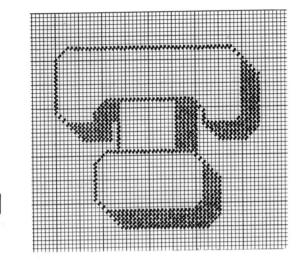

Letter R

1. Hungarian Stitch.
2. Algerian Eye Stitch in corners with Eyelet Stitch in center, Tent Stitch boxes.
3. Parisian Stitch.
4. Horizontal and vertical Straight Gobelin Stitch, worked over Tramé; Back Stitch between outer rows.
5. Tent Stitch with Slanting Gobelin Stitches used at random to create rain effect.

Letter S

1. Alternate boxes of Tent and Mosaic Stitch.
2. Jacquard Stitch.
3. Rounded Wave Stitch.

Letter T

1. Leaf Stitch on Tent Stitch ground.
2. Central motif of Slanting Gobelin in two directions. Cross Stitch in center; Tent Stitch ground, Back Stitch on either side.
3. Continuous Mosaic Stitch.

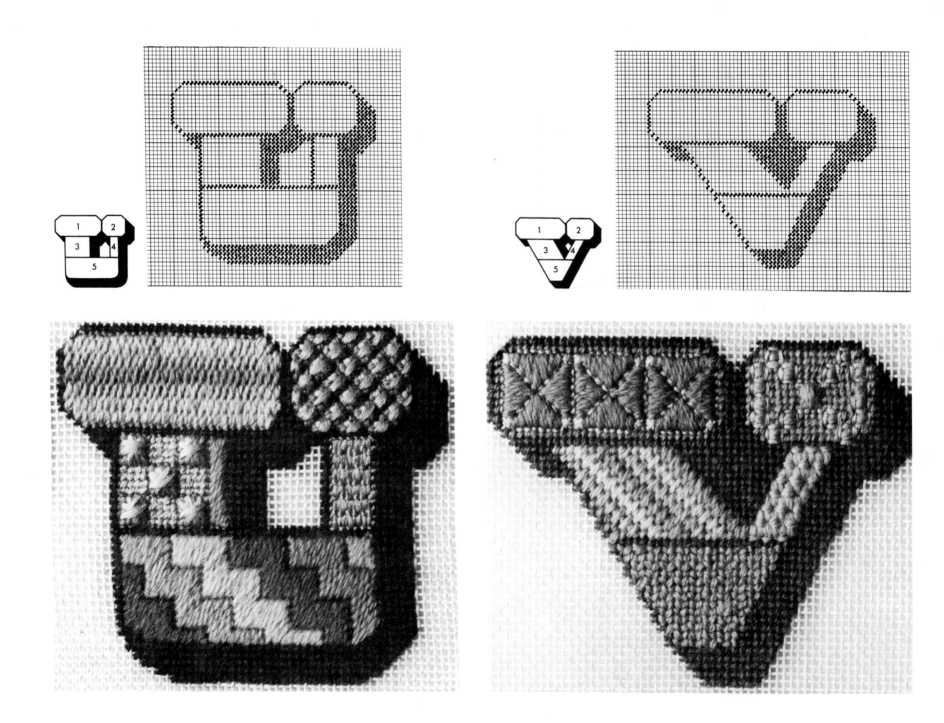

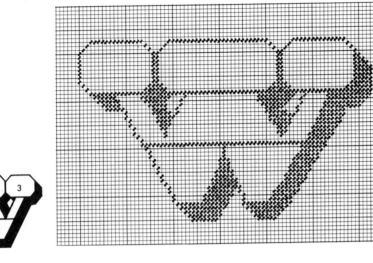

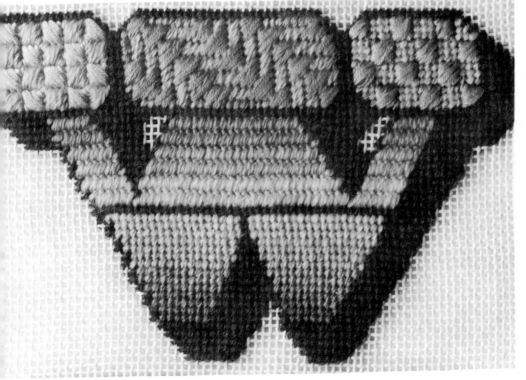

Letter U

1. Shaded Encroaching Gobelin Stitch with Back Stitch at top and bottom.
2. Double Cross Stitch.
3. Leviathan Stitch overstitched with Triple Cross Stitch; Tent Stitch panes.
4. French Stitch outlined with Back Stitch.
5. Byzantine Stitch.

Letter V

1. Triangle Stitch with Smyrna Stitch at corners; Back Stitch outlines.
2. Leviathan Stitch in center; Smyrna Stitch; Tent Stitch ground; Back Stitch outlines.
3. Continuous Mosaic Stitch.
4. Double and Tie Stitch.
5. Reversed Tent Stitch.

Letter W

1. Cushion Stitch.
2. Oriental Stitch.
3. Large Chequer Stitch; Flat Stitch portion overstitched in silk.
4. Slanting Gobelin Stitch, Back Stitch between rows.
5. Blended horizontal Tent Stitch.
6. Blended horizontal Tent Stitch.

135

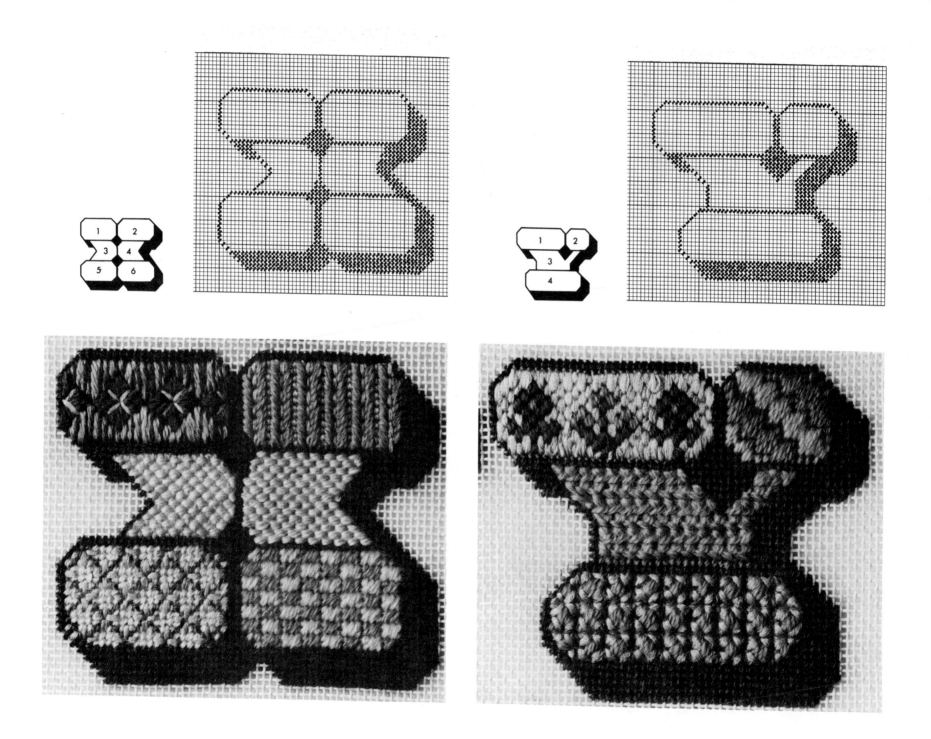

Letter X

1. Hungarian Stitches form diamonds, Slanting Gobelin x's; Bargello worked in one color and overstitched in contrasting color at top and bottom.
2. Stem Stitch.
3. Upright Cross Stitch.
4. Horizontal rows of Back Stitch.
5. Reversed Tent Stitch, Back Stitched at intersections.
6. Horizontal Cashmere Stitch.

Letter Y

1. Bargello.
2. Moorish Stitch.
3. Long-armed Cross Stitch.
4. Crossed Corners Stitch with Back Stitch between rows.

Letter Z

1. Milanese Stitch.
2. Hungarian Stitch.
3. Bargello.

Bibliography

Cox, Hebe, *Canvas Embroidery*, London, Mills and Boon Ltd., 1960.

de Dillmont, Therese, *Encyclopedia of Needlework*, France, D.M.C. Library.

Gibbon, M. A., *Canvas Work*, London, G. G. Bell and Sons Ltd., 1965.

Hanley, Hope, *Needlepoint*, New York, Charles Scribner's Sons, 1964.

King, Bucky, *Creative Canvas Embroidery*, New York, Hearthside Press Inc., 1963.

Lane, Maggie, *Needlepoint by Design*, New York, Charles Scribner's Sons, 1970.

Snook, Barbara, *Florentine Embroidery*, New York, Charles Scribner's Sons, 1967.

Thomas, Mary, *Dictionary of Embroidery Stitches*, London, Hodder and Stooughton Ltd., 1965.

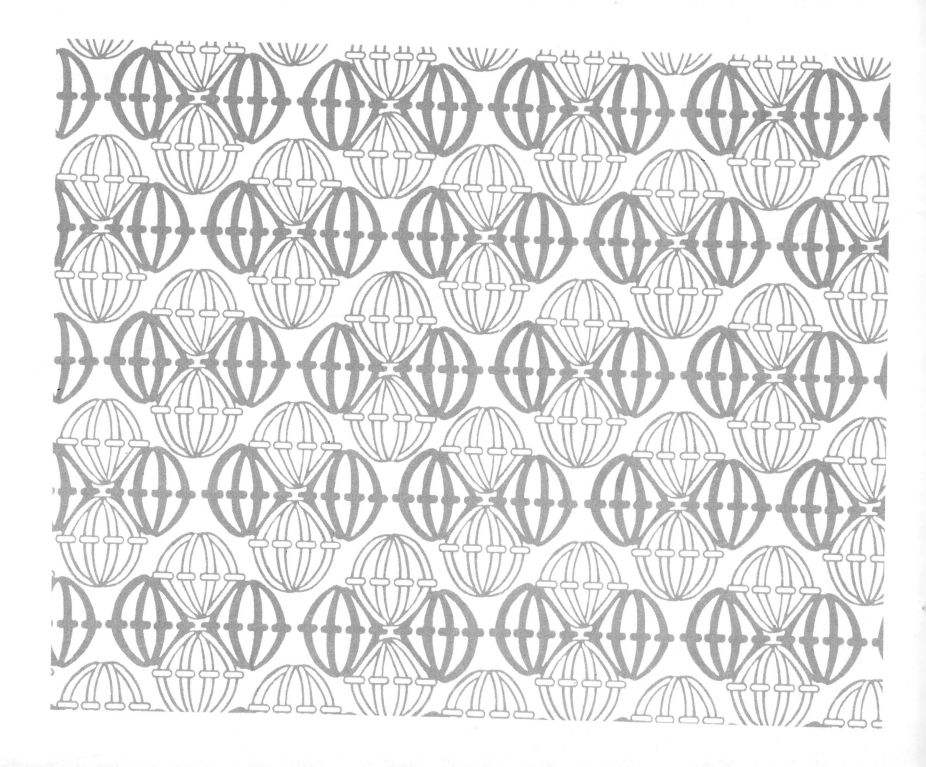

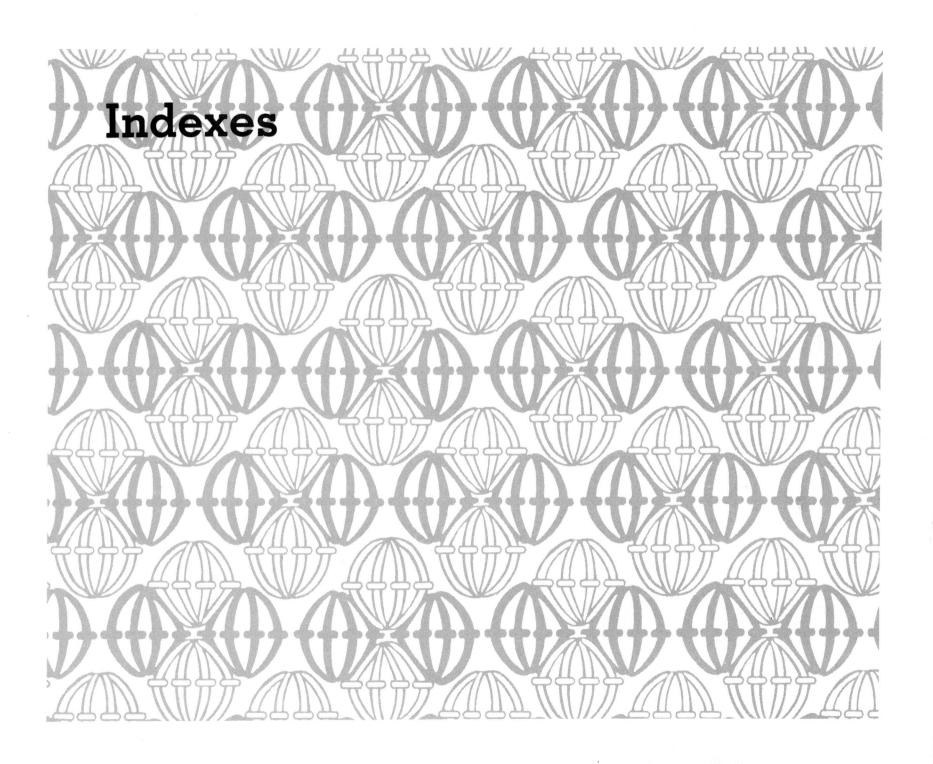

Indexes

Stitch Index

Index